THE ELOQUENT WAR
Personal and Public Writings from the Civil War

Edited by

Donna Bodden
and
Eleanor Lang

BRANDYWINE PRESS • St. James, New York

ISBN 1-881089-31-2

1st Printing

Telephone Orders: 1-800-345-1776

TABLE OF CONTENTS

SECTION ONE: 1860-1861

SECTION TWO: 1862

SECTION THREE: 1863

SECTION FOUR: 1864–1865

INTRODUCTION

With the Civil War, all Americans faced the weightiest moral and political issues since the American Revolution. They argued and agonized with themselves in diaries and journals, and with others in sermons, speeches, poems, and love letters. As they sought with words to hold their experiences steady for a moment, they sometimes achieved the eloquence that only comes in extraordinary times.

In these selections, written between 1860 and 1865, the experience of the war is immediate, unfiltered by memory. Passion is the genesis, felicity of phrasing is the form, and revelation is the result, making argument and experience tangible. It is a picture of the American family in the narrowest and broadest meaning of that phrase, a literature that crosses all social borders, an integrated portrait of the Civil War as a national experience.

Please note that the selections preserve the spelling, punctuation, and capitalization of the sources.

SECTION 1 1860–1861

Slavery and states' rights are the two central issues of the Civil War. In 1860 much of the agrarian southern economy depended on slave labor while the industrialized North offered technology and a market for southern goods. About four million slaves lived and worked in the United States in 1860, and the institution of slavery reverberated with political, social, economic, and moral implications.

Abraham Lincoln disapproved of the expansion of slavery. When it became apparent that he was going to win the presidential election of 1860, several southern states planned to secede. Believing that states should maintain their own autonomy and despising interference by a central government in their domestic affairs, South Carolina, Mississippi, Florida, Alabama, Georgia, Louisiana, and Texas left the Union. As the Confederate States of America, these seven states elected Jefferson Davis as their president. Virginia, Arkansas, North Carolina, and Tennessee also wanted to guarantee their independence and institutions such as slavery in their states and joined the Confederacy later in 1861.

Tension and hysteria escalated between the North and the South over secession. Although the Confederacy claimed each state's sovereignty, Lincoln, in his first inaugural address in 1861, advocated a compromise and exhorted the nation to avoid war. But events at Fort Sumter in South Carolina ignited a war fever throughout the country, for after Lincoln ordered supplies to be sent in to the federal troops occupying the fort, the Confederate government demanded its surrender. On April 12, 1861 the first shot was fired on Fort Sumter by a Confederate soldier and the Union surrendered after thirty-four hours of fighting. Thousands of men entered the ranks of both the Union and the Confederate armies. The first great battle of the Civil War, the Battle of Bull Run, began on July 21, 1861. In northern Virginia, the new and amateur Union army attacked and, to its surprise, did not defeat the disorganized Confederate forces.

Sentiments on slavery and secession were not always so clearly divided between North and South. As the following selections demonstrate, not all Unionists lived in the North, free blacks were not assured of civil rights, white preachers and black activists blamed the North as well as the South for slavery, and even the most patriotic soldiers harbored doubts about a war between citizens.

HERMAN MELVILLE

Ten years after Herman Melville published Moby Dick, *his grand and ferocious fictional view of the dark side of human existence, the coming storm of the Civil War verified his terrible vision for the once optimistic republic.*

MISGIVINGS
(1860)

When ocean-clouds over inland hills
  Sweep storming in late autumn brown,
And horror the sodden valley fills,
  And the spire falls crashing in the town,
I muse upon my country's ills—
The tempest bursting from the waste of Time
On the world's fairest hope linked with man's foulest
    crime.

Nature's dark side is heeded now—
  (Ah! optimist-cheer disheartened flown)—
A child may read the moody brow
  Of yon black mountain lone.
With shouts the torrents down the gorges go,
And storms are formed behind the storm we feel:
The hemlock shakes in the rafter, the oak in the driv-
    ing keel.

SOURCE: *Battle-Pieces and Aspects of the War*
(New York, 1866).

SARAH LOGUE

The ultimate impossibility of democracy co-existing with slavery is dramatized in an exchange of letters between a Tennessee slave owner, Sarah Logue, and Jarmain Wesley Loguen, who has liberated himself from her owner-

ship. Juxtaposed, these two letters reveal the radically different meanings each gives to such terms as private property, theft, freedom, human rights, and reciprocity.

LETTER TO REV. J. W. LOGUEN, FROM HIS OLD MISTRESS

Maury Co., State of Tennessee
February 20th, 1860

To JARM:— . . . I write you these lines to let you know the situation we are in,—partly in consequence of your running away and stealing Old Rock, our fine mare. Though we got the mare back, she was never worth much after you took her;— and, as I now stand in need of some funds, I have determined to sell you; and I have had an offer for you, but did not see fit to take it. If you will send me one thousand dollars, and pay for the old mare, I will give up all claim I have to you. Write to me as soon as you get these lines, and let me know if you will accept my proposition. In consequence of your running away, we had to sell Abe and Ann and twelve acres of land; and I want you to send me the money, that I may be able to redeem the land that you was the cause of our selling, and on receipt of the above-named sum of money, I will send you your bill of sale. If you do not comply with my request, I will sell you to some one else. . . .

I understand that you are a preacher. . . . I would like to know if you read your Bible. If so, can you tell what will become of the thief if he does not repent? and, if the blind lead the blind, what will the consequence be? . . . You know that we reared you as we reared our own children; that you was never abused, and that shortly before you ran away, when your master asked you if you would like to be sold, you said you would not leave him to go with any body.

SARAH LOGUE.

JARMAIN WESLEY LOGUEN

MR. LOGUEN'S REPLY

Syracuse, (N.Y.) March 28, 1860

MRS. SARAH LOGUE: . . .You sold my brother and sister, Abe and Ann, and twelve acres of land, you say, because I ran away. Now you have the unutterable meanness to ask me to return and be your miserable chattel, or, in lieu thereof, send you $1000 to enable you to redeem the *land*, but not to redeem my poor brother and sister! If I were to send you money, it would be to get my brother and sister, and not that you should get land. You say you are *cripple*, and doubtless you say it to stir my pity, for you know I was susceptible in that direction. I do pity you from the bottom of my heart. Nevertheless, I am indignant beyond the power of words to express, that you should be so sunken and cruel as to tear the hearts I love so much all in pieces; that you should be willing to impale and crucify us all, out of compassion for your poor *foot* or *leg*. Wretched woman! Be it known to you that I value my freedom, to say nothing of my mother, brothers and sisters, more than your whole body; more, indeed, than my own life; more than all the lives of all the slaveholders and tyrants under heaven.

You say you have offers to buy me, and that you shall sell me if I do not send you $1000, and in the same breath and almost in the same sentence, you say, 'You know we raised you as we did our own children.' Woman, did you raise your *own children* for the market? Did you raise them for the whipping-post? Did you raise them to be driven off, bound to a coffle in chains? Where are my poor bleeding brothers and sisters? Can you tell? Who was it that sent them off into sugar and cotton fields, to be kicked and cuffed, and whipped, and to groan and die; and where no kin can hear their groans, or attend and sympathize at their dying bed, or follow in their funeral? . . .

But you say I am a thief, because I took the old mare along with me. Have you got to learn that I had a better right to the old mare, as you call her, than Manasseth Logue had to me? Is it a greater sin for me to steal his horse, than it was for him to rob my mother's cradle, and steal me? If he and you infer that I forfeit all my rights to you, shall not I infer that you forfeit all your rights to me? Have you got to learn that human rights are mutual and reciprocal, and if you take my liberty and life, you forfeit your own liberty and life? Before God and high heaven, is there a law for one man which is not a law for every other man?

If you or any other speculator on my body and rights, wish to know how I regard my rights, they need but come here, and lay their hands on me to enslave me. Do you think to terrify me by presenting the alternative to give my money to you, or give my body to slavery? Then let me say to you, that I meet the proposition with unutterable scorn and contempt. The proposition is an outrage and an insult. I will not budge one hair's breadth. . . . I stand among a free people, who, I thank God, sympathize with my rights, and the rights of mankind; and if your emissaries and venders come here to re-enslave me, and escape the unshrinking vigor of my own right arm, I trust my strong and brave friends, in this city and State, will be my rescuers and avengers.

Yours, &c., J. W. LOGUEN.

Source: *The Liberator*, April 27, 1860.

THE REVEREND BENJAMIN PALMER

In a two-hour sermon, the Reverend Benjamin Palmer gives the definitive defense of slavery on moral, political, and economic grounds, asserting along the way the superiority of the southern land-based hierarchical culture. These portions of that sermon highlight his major arguments and give the reader a sense of the moral passion that supporters of the Confederacy brought to their cause.

THANKSGIVING SERMON
November 29, 1860

First Presbyterian Church   New Orleans

... A nation often has a character as well defined and intense as that of an individual. ... [H]owever derived, this individuality of character alone makes any people truly historic. ... If then the South is such a people, what, at this juncture, is their providential trust? I answer, that it is *to conserve and to perpetuate the institution of domestic slavery as now existing*. It is not necessary here to inquire whether this is precisely the best relation in which the hewer of wood and drawer of water can stand to his employer; although this proposition may perhaps be successfully sustained by those who choose to defend it. Still less are we required, dogmatically, to affirm that it will subsist through all time. Baffled as our wisdom may now be in finding a solution of this intricate social problem, it would nevertheless be the height of arrogance to pronounce what changes may or may not occur in the distant future. In the grand march of events Providence may work out a solution undiscoverable by us. What modifications of soil and climate may hereafter be produced, what consequent changes in the products on which we depend, what political revolutions may occur among the races which are now enacting the great drama of history: all such inquiries are totally irrelevant because no prophetic vision can pierce the darkness of that future. If this question should ever arise, the generation to whom it is remitted will doubtless have the wisdom to meet it, and Providence will furnish the lights in which it is to be resolved. All that we claim for them, for ourselves, is liberty to work out this problem, guided by nature and God, without obtrusive interference from abroad. These great questions of Providence and history must have free scope for their solution; and the race whose fortunes are distinctly implicated in the same is alone authorized, as it is alone competent, to determine them. It is just this impertinence of human legislation, setting bounds to what God alone can regulate, that the South is called this day to resent and resist. The country is convulsed simply because 'the throne of iniquity frameth mischief by a law.' Without, therefore, determining the question of duty for future generations, I simply say, that for us, as now situated, the duty is plain of conserving and transmitting the system of slavery, with the freest scope for its natural development and extension. Let us, my brethren, look our duty in the face. With this institution assigned to our keeping, what reply shall we make to those who say that its days are numbered? My own conviction is, that we should at once lift ourselves, intelligently, to the highest moral ground and proclaim to all the world that we hold this trust from God, and in its occupancy we are prepared to stand or fall as God may appoint. If the critical moment has arrived at which the great issue is joined, let us say that, in the sight of all perils, we will stand by our trust; and God be with the right!

The argument which enforces the solemnity of this providential trust is simple and condensed. It is bound upon us, then, by the *principle of self-preservation*, that 'first law' which is continually asserting its supremacy over all others. Need I pause to show how this system of servitude underlies and supports our material interests; that our wealth consists in our lands and in the serfs who till them; that from the nature of our products they can only be cultivated by labor which must be controlled in order to be certain; that any other than a tropical race must faint and wither beneath a tropical sun? Need I pause to show how this system is interwoven with our entire social fabric; that these slaves form parts of our households, even as our children; and that, too, through a relationship recognized and sanctioned in the Scriptures of God even as the other? Must I pause to show how it has fashioned our modes of life, and determined all our habits of thought and feeling, and moulded the very type of our civilization? How then can the hand of violence be laid upon it without involving our existence? The so-called free States of this country are working out the social problem under conditions peculiar to themselves. These conditions are sufficiently hard, and their success is too uncertain to excite in us the least jealousy of their lot. With a teeming population, which the soil cannot support; with their wealth depending upon arts, created by artificial wants; with an external friction between the grades of their society; with their labor and their capital grinding against each other like the upper and nether millstones; with labor cheapened and displaced by new mechanical inventions, bursting more asunder the bonds of brotherhood—amid these intricate perils we have ever given them our sympathy and our prayers, and have never sought to weaken the foundations of their social order. God grant them complete success in the solution of all their perplexities! . . .

This duty is bound upon us again *as the constituted guardians of the slaves themselves.* Our lot is not more implicated in theirs, than their lot in ours; in our mutual relations we survive or perish together. . . . My servant, whether born in my house or bought with my money, stands to me in the relation of a child. Though providentially owing me service, which, providentially, I am bound to exact, he is, nevertheless, my brother and my friend, and I am to him a guardian and a father. He leans upon me for protection, for counsel, and for blessing; and so long as the relation continues, no power but the power of Almighty God shall come between him and me. Were there no argument but this, it binds upon us the providential duty of preserving the relation that we may save him from a doom worse than death.

It is a duty which we owe, further, *to the civilized world.* It is a remarkable fact that during these thirty years of unceasing warfare against slavery, and while a lying spirit has inflamed the world against us, that world has grown more and more dependent upon it for sustenance and wealth. Every tyro knows that all branches of industry fall back upon the soil. We must come, every one of us, to the bosom of this great mother for nourishment. In the happy partnership which has grown up in providence between the tribes of this confederacy, our industry has been concentrated upon agriculture. To the North we have cheerfully resigned all the profits arising from manufacture and commerce. Those profits they have, for the most part, fairly earned, and we have never begrudged them. . . .

[I]n this great struggle, *we defend the cause of God and religion.* The abolition spirit is undeniably atheistic. . . . Among a people so generally religious as the American, a disguise must be worn; but it is the same old threadbare disguise of the advocacy of human rights. . . . [T]he decree has gone forth which strikes at God by striking at all subordination and law. Availing itself of the morbid and misdirected sympathies of men, it has entrapped weak consciences in the meshes of its treachery; and now, at last, has seated its high priest upon the throne, clad in the black garments of discord and schism, so symbolic of its ends. Under this suspicious cry of reform, it demands that every evil shall be corrected, or society become a wreck—the sun must be stricken from the heavens, if a spot is found upon his disk. The Most High, knowing his own power, which is infinite, and his own wisdom, which is unfathomable, can afford to be patient. But these self-consti-tuted reformers must quicken the activity of Jehovah or compel his ab-dication. In their furious haste, they trample upon obligations sacred as any which can bind the conscience. It is time to reproduce the ob-solete idea that Providence must govern man, and not that man shall control Providence. In the imperfect state of human society, it pleases God to allow evils which check others that are greater. As in the phys-ical world, objects are moved forward, not by a single force, but by the composition of forces; so in his moral administration, there are checks and balances whose intimate relations are comprehended only by himself. But what reck they of this—these fierce zealots who under-take to drive the chariot of the sun? Working out the single and false idea which rides them like a nightmare, they dash athwart the spheres, utterly disregarding the delicate mechanism of Providence, which moves on, wheels within wheels, with pivots and balances and springs, which the great Designer alone can control. This spirit of atheism, which knows no God who tolerates evil, no Bible which sanctions law, and no conscience that can be bound by oaths and covenants, has se-lected us for its victims, and slavery for its issue. Its banner-cry rings out already upon the air—'liberty, equality, fraternity,' which simply in-terpreted mean bondage, confiscation and massacre. . . .

SOURCE: *The Life and Letters of
Benjamin Morgan Palmer*
(Richmond, Va., 1906).

HARRIET JACOBS

For southern black women, a private war had been go-ing on long before the war between the states. That war involved their sexually predatory masters and their jeal-ous mistresses. In her 1861 book, Incidents in the Life of a Slave Girl, *Harriet Jacobs reenacts the autobiograph-ical drama. She also perceives the hypocrisy of the North condemning slavery yet allowing fugitive slaves to be re-turned and of some northern families for encouraging their daughters to marry slaveholders.*

THE JEALOUS MISTRESS

I would ten thousand times rather that my children should be the half-starved paupers of Ireland than to be the most pampered among the slaves of America. I would rather drudge out my life on a cotton plantation, till the grave opened to give me rest, than to live with an unprincipled master and a jealous mistress. The felon's home in a penitentiary is preferable. He may repent, and turn from the error of his ways, and so find peace; but it is not so with a favorite slave. She is not allowed to have any pride of character. It is deemed a crime in her to wish to be virtuous.

Mrs. Flint possessed the key to her husband's character before I was born. She might have used this knowledge to counsel and to screen the young and the innocent among her slaves; but for them she had no sympathy. They were the objects of her constant suspicion and malevolence. She watched her husband with unceasing vigilance; but he was well practised in means to evade it. What he could not find opportunity to say in words he manifested in signs. He invented more than were ever thought of in a deaf and dumb asylum. I let them pass, as if I did not understand what he meant; and many were the curses and threats bestowed on me for my stupidity. One day he caught me teaching myself to write. He frowned, as if he was not well pleased; but I suppose he came to the conclusion that such an accomplishment might help to advance his favorite scheme. Before long, notes were often slipped into my hand. I would return them, saying, "I can't read them, sir." "Can't you?" he replied; "then I must read them to you." He always finished the reading by asking, "Do you understand?" Sometimes he would complain of the heat of the tea room, and order his supper to be placed on a small table in the piazza. He would seat himself there with a well-satisfied smile, and tell me to stand by and brush away the flies. He would eat very slowly, pausing between the mouthfuls. These intervals were employed in describing the happiness I was so foolishly throwing away, and in threatening me with the penalty that finally awaited my stubborn disobedience. He boasted much of the forbearance he had exercised towards me, and reminded me that there was a limit to his patience. When I succeeded in avoiding opportunities for him to talk to me at home, I was ordered to come to his office, to do some errand. When there, I was obliged to stand and listen to such language as he saw fit to address to me. Sometimes I so openly expressed my contempt for him that he would become violently enraged, and I wondered why he did not strike me. Circumstanced as he was, he probably thought it was better policy to be forbearing. But the state of things grew worse and worse daily. In desperation I told him that I must and would apply to my grandmother for protection. He threatened me with death, and worse than death, if I made any complaint to her. Strange to say, I did not despair. I was naturally of a buoyant disposition, and always I had a hope of somehow getting out of his clutches. Like many a poor, simple slave before me, I trusted that some threads of joy would yet be woven into my dark destiny.

I had entered my sixteenth year, and every day it became more apparent that my presence was intolerable to Mrs. Flint. Angry words frequently passed between her and her husband. He had never punished me himself, and he would not allow any body else to punish me. In that respect, she was never satisfied; but, in her angry moods, no terms were too vile for her to bestow upon me. Yet I, whom she detested so bitterly, had far more pity for her than he had, whose duty it was to make her life happy. I never wronged her, or wished to wrong her; and one word of kindness from her would have brought me to her feet.

After repeated quarrels between the doctor and his wife, he announced his intention to take his youngest daughter, then four years old, to sleep in his apartment. It was necessary that a servant should sleep in the same room, to be on hand if the child stirred. I was selected for that office, and informed for what purpose that arrangement had been made. By managing to keep within sight of people, as much as possible, during the day time, I had hitherto succeeded in eluding my master, though a razor was often held to my throat to force me to change this line of policy. At night I slept by the side of my great aunt, where I felt safe. He was too prudent to come into her room. She was an old woman, and had been in the family many years. Moreover, as a married man, and a professional man, he deemed it necessary to save appearances in some degree. But he resolved to remove the obstacle in the way of his scheme; and he thought he had planned it so that he should evade suspicion. He was well aware how much I prized my refuge by the side of my old aunt, and he determined to dispossess me of it. The first night the doctor had the little child in his room alone. The next morning, I was ordered to take my station as nurse the following night. A kind Providence interposed in my favor. During the day Mrs. Flint heard of this new arrangement, and a storm followed. I rejoiced to hear it rage.

After a while my mistress sent for me to come to her room. Her first question was, "Did you know you were to sleep in the doctor's room?"

"Yes ma'am."

"Who told you."

"My master."

"Will you answer truly all the questions I ask?"

"Yes ma'am."

"Tell me, then, as you hope to be forgiven, are you innocent of what I have accused you?"

"I am."

She handed me a Bible, and said, "Lay your hand on your heart, kiss this holy book, and swear before God that you tell me the truth."

I took the oath she required, and I did it with a clear conscience.

"You have taken God's holy word to testify your innocence," said she. "If you have deceived me, beware! Now take this stool, sit down, look me directly in the face, and tell me all that has passed between your master and you."

I did as she ordered. As I went on with my account her color changed frequently, she wept, and sometimes groaned. She spoke in tones so sad, that I was touched by her grief. The tears came to my eyes; but I was soon convinced that her emotions arose from anger and wounded pride. She felt that her marriage vows were desecrated, her dignity insulted; but she had no compassion for the poor victim of her husband's perfidy. She pitied herself as a martyr; but she was incapable of feeling for the condition of shame and misery in which her unfortunate, helpless slave was placed.

Yet perhaps she had some touch of feeling for me; for when the conference was ended, she spoke kindly, and promised to protect me. I should have been much comforted by this assurance if I could have had confidence in it; but my experiences in slavery had filled me with distrust. She was not a very refined woman, and had not much control over her passions. I was an object of her jealousy, and, consequently, of her hatred; and I knew I could not expect kindness or confidence from her under the circumstances in which I was placed. I could not blame her. Slaveholders' wives feel as other women would under similar circumstances. The fire of her temper kindled from small sparks, and now the flame became so intense that the doctor was obliged to give up his intended arrangement.

I knew I had ignited the torch, and I expected to suffer for it afterwards; but I felt too thankful to my mistress for the timely aid she rendered me to care much about that. She now took me to sleep in a room adjoining her own. There I was an object of her especial care, though not of her especial comfort, for she spent many a sleepless night to watch over me. Sometimes I woke up, and found her bending over me. At other times she whispered in my ear, as though it was her husband who was speaking to me, and listened to hear what I would answer. If she startled me, on such occasions, she would glide stealthily away; and the next morning she would tell me I had been talking in my sleep, and ask who I was talking to. At last, I began to be fearful for my life. It had been often threatened; and you can imagine, better than I can describe, what an unpleasant sensation it must produce to wake up in the dead of night and find a jealous woman bending over you. Terrible as this experience was, I had fears that it would give place to one more terrible.

My mistress grew weary of her vigils; they did not prove satisfactory. She changed her tactics. She now tried the trick of accusing my master of crime, in my presence, and gave my name as the author of the accusation. To my utter astonishment, he replied, "I don't believe it; but if she did acknowledge it, you tortured her into exposing me." Tortured into exposing him! Truly, Satan had no difficulty in distinguishing the color of his soul! I understood his object in making this false representation. It was to show me that I gained nothing by seeking the protection of my mistress; that the power was still all in his own hands. I pitied Mrs. Flint. She was a second wife, many years the junior of her husband; and the hoary-headed miscreant was enough to try the patience of a wiser and better woman. She was completely foiled, and knew not how to proceed. She would gladly have had me flogged for my supposed false oath; but, as I have already stated, the doctor never allowed any one to whip me. The old sinner was politic. The application of the lash might have led to remarks that would have exposed him in the eyes of his children and grandchildren. How often did I rejoice that I lived in a town where all the inhabitants knew each other! If I had been on a remote plantation, or lost among the multitude of a crowded city, I should not be a living woman at this day.

The secrets of slavery are concealed like those of the Inquisition. My master was, to my knowledge, the father of eleven slaves. But did the mothers dare to tell who was the father of their children? Did the other slaves dare to allude to it, except in whispers among themselves? No, indeed! They knew too well the terrible consequences.

My grandmother could not avoid seeing things which excited her suspicions. She was uneasy about me, and tried various ways to buy me; but the never-changing answer was always repeated: "Linda does not belong to *me*. She is my daughter's property, and I have no legal right to sell her." The conscientious man! He was too scrupulous to *sell* me; but he had no scruples whatever about committing a much greater wrong against the helpless young girl placed under his guardianship, as his daughter's property. Sometimes my persecutor would ask me whether I would like to be sold. I told him I would rather be sold to any body than to lead such a life as I did. On such occasions he would assume the air of a very injured individual, and reproach me for my ingratitude. "Did I not take you into the house, and make you the companion of my own children?" he would say. "Have I ever treated you like a negro? I have never allowed you to be punished, not even to please your mistress. And this is the recompense I get, you ungrateful girl!" I answered that he had reasons of his own for screening me from punishment, and that the course he pursued made my mistress hate me and persecute me. If I wept, he would say, "Poor child! Don't cry! don't cry! I will make peace for you with your mistress. Only let me arrange matters in my own way. Poor, foolish girl! you don't know what is for your own good. I would cherish you. I would make a lady of you. Now go, and think of all I have promised you."

I did think of it.

Reader, I draw no imaginary pictures of southern homes. I am telling you the plain truth. Yet when victims make their escape from this wild beast of Slavery, northerners consent to act the part of bloodhounds, and hunt the poor fugitive back into his den, "full of dead men's bones, and all uncleanness." Nay, more, they are not only willing, but proud, to give their daughters in marriage to slaveholders. The poor girls have romantic notions of a sunny clime, and of the flowering vines that all the year round shade a happy home. To what disappointments are they destined! The young wife soon learns that the husband in whose hands she has placed her happiness pays no regard to his marriage vows. Children of every shade of complexion play with her own fair babies, and too well she knows that they are born unto him of his own household. Jealousy and hatred enter the flowery home, and it is ravaged of its loveliness.

Southern women often marry a man knowing that he is the father of many little slaves. They do not trouble themselves about it. They regard such children as property, as marketable as the pigs on the plantation; and it is seldom that they do not make them aware of this by passing them into the slave-trader's hands as soon as possible, and thus getting them out of their sight. I am glad to say there are some honorable exceptions.

I have myself known two southern wives who exhorted their husbands to free those slaves towards whom they stood in a "parental relation;" and their request was granted. These husbands blushed before the superior nobleness of the wives' natures. Though they had only counselled them to do that which it was their duty to do, it commanded their respect, and rendered their conduct more exemplary. Concealment was at an end, and confidence took the place of distrust.

Though this bad institution deadens the moral sense, even in white women, to a fearful extent, it is not altogether extinct. I have heard southern ladies say of Mr. Such a one, "He not only thinks it no disgrace to be the father of those little niggers, but he is not ashamed to call himself their master. I declare, such things ought not to be tolerated in any decent society!"

SOURCE: Harriet Jacobs, *Incidents in the Life of a Slave Girl*, edited by L. Maria Child (Boston, 1861).

ABRAHAM LINCOLN

Abraham Lincoln took the oath of office as President of the United States three weeks after Jefferson Davis had taken his as President of the Confederate States of Amer-

ica. In swearing to uphold the Constitution, Lincoln makes it clear that he understands what that oath means: protection of the property rights of slave owners as well as the preservation of the Union.

FIRST INAUGURAL ADDRESS
March 4, 1861

. . . One section of our country believes slavery is right, and ought to be extended, while the other believes it is wrong, and ought not to be extended. This is the only substantial dispute. The fugitive slave clause of the Constitution, and the law for the suppression of the foreign slave-trade, are each as well enforced, perhaps, as any law can ever be in a community where the moral sense of the people imperfectly supports the law itself. The great body of the people abide by the dry legal obligation in both cases, and a few break over in each. This, I think, cannot be perfectly cured; and it would be worse, in both cases, after the separation of the sections than before. The foreign slave trade, now imperfectly suppressed, would be ultimately revived, without restriction, in one section; while fugitive slaves, now only partially surrendered, would not be surrendered at all by the other.

Physically speaking, we cannot separate. We cannot remove our respective sections from each other, nor build an impassable wall between them. A husband and wife may be divorced, and go out of the presence and beyond the reach of each other; but the different parts of our country cannot do this. They cannot but remain face to face; and intercourse, either amicable or hostile, must continue between them. It is impossible, then, to make that intercourse more advantageous or more satisfactory after separation than before. Can aliens make treaties easier than friends can make laws? Can treaties be more faithfully enforced between aliens than laws can among friends? Suppose you go to war, you cannot fight always; and when, after much loss on both sides, and no gain on either, you cease fighting, the identical old questions, as to terms of intercourse, are again upon you. . . .

My countrymen, one and all, think calmly and well upon this whole subject. Nothing valuable can be lost by taking time. If there be an object to hurry any of you in hot haste to a step which you would never take deliberately, that object will be frustrated by taking time; but no good object can be frustrated by it. Such of you as are now dissatisfied, still have the old Constitution unimpaired, and, on the sensitive point, the laws of your own framing under it; while the new Administration will have no immediate power, if it would, to change either. If it were admitted that you who are dissatisfied hold the right side in the dispute, there still is no single good reason for precipitate action. Intelligence, patriotism, Christianity, and a firm reliance on Him who has never yet forsaken this favored land, are still competent to adjust, in the best way, all our present difficulty.

In your hands, my dissatisfied fellow-countrymen, and not in mine, is the momentous issue of civil war. The Government will not assail you.

You can have no conflict without being yourselves the aggressors. You have no oath registered in Heaven to destroy the Government; while I shall have the most solemn one to "preserve, protect and defend" it.

I am loth to close. We are not enemies, but friends. We must not be enemies. Though passion may have strained, it must not break our bonds of affection.

The mystic chords of memory, stretching from every battle-field and patriot grave to every living heart and hearthstone all over this broad land, will yet swell the chorus of the Union, when again touched, as surely they will be, by the better angels of our nature.

SOURCE: *The Life and Public Services of Abraham Lincoln* by Henry J. Raymond (New York, 1865).

ANONYMOUS*

For civilians trapped behind enemy lines, isolation defined their lives. In the secret diary that records with vivid metaphors her dissent from the Confederate fervor, this northern-born wife of a southern gentleman maintains her national values and patriotic identity. Like the nation, she finds herself caught between old loyalties and the new hysteria.

WAR DIARY OF A UNION WOMAN IN THE SOUTH

I
SECESSION

New Orleans, Dec. 1, 1860.—I understand it now. Keeping journals is for those who cannot, or dare not, speak out. So I shall set up a journal, being only a rather lonely young girl in a very small and hated mi-

---

*After the war, the author was identified as Mrs. Dora Richards Miller.

nority. On my return here in November, after a foreign voyage and absence of many months, I found myself behind in knowledge of the political conflict, but heard the dread sounds of disunion and war muttered in threatening tones. Surely no native-born woman loves her country better than I love America. The blood of one of its Revolutionary patriots flows in my veins, and it is the Union for which he pledged his "life, fortune, and sacred honor" that I love, not any divided or special section of it. So I have been reading attentively and seeking light from foreigners and natives on all questions at issue. Living from birth in slave countries, both foreign and American, and passing through one slave insurrection in early childhood, the saddest and also the pleasantest features of slavery have been familiar. If the South goes to war for slavery, slavery is doomed in this country. To say so is like opposing one drop to a roaring torrent. . . .

Jan. 26, 1861.—The solemn boom of cannon to-day announced that the convention have passed the ordinance of secession. We must take a reef in our patriotism and narrow it down to State limits. Mine still sticks out all around the borders of the State. It will be bad if New Orleans should secede from Louisiana and set up for herself. Then indeed I would be "cabined, cribbed, confined." The faces in the house are jubilant to-day. Why is it so easy for them and not for me to "ring out the old, ring in the new"? I am out of place.

Jan. 28, *Monday.*—Sunday has now got to be a day of special excitement. The gentlemen save all the sensational papers to regale us with at the late Sunday breakfast. Rob opened the battle yesterday morning by saying to me in his most aggressive manner, "G., I believe these are your sentiments"; and then he read aloud an article from the "Journal des Debats" expressing in rather contemptuous terms the fact that France will follow the policy of non-intervention. When I answered, "Well, what do you expect? This is not their quarrel," he raved at me, ending by a declaration that he would willingly pay my passage to foreign parts if I would like to go. "Rob," said his father, "keep cool; don't let that threat excite you. Cotton is king. Just wait till they feel the pinch a little; their tone will change." I went to Trinity Church. Some Union people who are not Episcopalians go there now because the pastor has not so much chance to rail at the Lord when things are not going to suit. But yesterday was a marked Sunday. The usual prayer for the President and Congress was changed to the "governor and people of this commonwealth and their representatives in convention assembled."

The city was very lively and noisy this evening with rockets and lights in honor of secession. Mrs. F., in common with the neighbors, illuminated. We walked out to see the houses of others gleaming amid the dark shrubbery like a fairy scene. The perfect stillness added to the effect, while the moon rose slowly with calm splendor. We hastened home to dress for a soirée, but on the stairs Edith said, "G., first come and help me dress Phoebe and Chloe [the negro servants]. There is a ball to-night in aristocratic colored society. This is Chloe's first introduction to New Orleans circles, and Henry Judson, Phoebe's husband, gave five dollars for a ticket for her." Chloe is a recent purchase from Georgia. We superintended their very stylish toilets, and Edith said, "G., run into your room, please, and write a pass for Henry. Put Mr. D.'s name to it." "Why, Henry is free," I said. "That makes no difference; all colored people must have a pass if out late. They choose a master for protection, and always carry his pass. Henry chose Mr. D., but he's lost the pass he had."

II
THE VOLUNTEERS—FORT SUMTER

. . . *March* 10, 1861.—The excitement in this house has risen to fever-heat during the past week. The four gentlemen have each a different plan for saving the country, and . . . Lincoln's inauguration and the story of the disguise in which he traveled to Washington is a never-ending source of gossip. The family board being the common forum, each gentleman as he appears first unloads his pockets of papers from all the Southern States, and then his overflowing heart to his eager female listeners, who in turn relate, inquire, sympathize, or cheer. If I dare express a doubt that the path to victory will be a flowery one, eyes flash, cheeks burn, and tongues clatter, till all are checked up suddenly by a warning rap for "Order, order!" from the amiable lady presiding. Thus we swallow politics with every meal. We take a mouthful and read a telegram, one eye on table, the other on the paper. One must be made of cool stuff to keep calm and collected, but I say but little. This war fever has banished small talk. Through all the black servants move about quietly, never seeming to notice that this is all about them.

"How can you speak so plainly before them?" I say.

"Why, what matter? They know that we shall keep the whip-handle."

April 13, 1861.—More than a month has passed since the last date here. This afternoon I was seated on the floor covered with loveliest flowers, arranging a floral offering for the fair, when the gentlemen arrived and with papers bearing news of the fall of Fort Sumter, which, at her request, I read to Mrs. F.

April 20.—The last few days have glided away in a halo of beauty. But nobody has time or will to enjoy it. War, war! is the one idea. The children play only with toy cannons and soldiers; the oldest inhabitant goes by every day with his rifle to practice; the public squares are full of companies drilling, and are now the fashionable resorts. We have been told that it is best for women to learn how to shoot too, so as to protect themselves when the men have gone to battle. Every evening after dinner we adjourn to the back lot and fire at a target with pistols. Yesterday I dined at Uncle Ralph's. Some members of the bar were present, and were jubilant about their brand-new Confederacy. It would soon be the grandest government ever known. Uncle Ralph said solemnly, "No, gentlemen; the day we seceded the star of our glory set." The words sunk into my mind like a knell, and made me wonder at the mind that could recognize that and yet adhere to the doctrine of secession.

In the evening I attended a farewell gathering at a friend's whose brothers are to leave this week for Richmond. There was music. No minor chord was permitted.

III
TRIBULATION

April 25.—Yesterday I went with Cousin E. to have her picture taken. The picture-galleries are doing a thriving business. Many companies are ordered off to take possession of Fort Pickens (Florida), and all seem to be leaving sweethearts behind them. The crowd was in high spirits; they don't dream that any destinies will be spoiled. When I got home Edith was reading from the daily paper of the dismissal of Miss G. from her place as teacher for expressing abolition sentiments, and that she would be ordered to leave the city. Soon a lady came with a paper setting forth that she has established a "company"—we are nothing if not military—for making lint and getting stores of linen to supply the hospitals.

My name went down. If it had n't, my spirit would have been wounded as with sharp spears before night. Next came a little girl with a subscription paper to get a flag for a certain company. The little girls, especially the pretty ones, are kept busy trotting around with subscription lists. Latest of all came little Guy, Mr. F.'s youngest clerk, the pet of the firm as well as of his home, a mere boy of sixteen. Such senseless sacrifices seem a sin. He chattered brightly, but lingered about, saying good-by. He got through it bravely until Edith's husband incautiously said, "You did n't kiss your little sweetheart," as he always called Ellie, who had been allowed to sit up. He turned and suddenly broke into agonizing sobs and then ran down the steps.

May 10.—I am tired and ashamed of myself. Last week I attended a meeting of the lint society to hand in the small contribution of linen

I had been able to gather. We scraped lint till it was dark. A paper was shown, entitled the "Volunteer's Friend," started by the girls of the high school, and I was asked to help the girls with it. I positively declined. To-day I was pressed into service to make red flannel cartridge-bags for ten-inch columbiads. I basted while Mrs. S. sewed, and I felt ashamed to think that I had not the moral courage to say, "I don't approve of your war and won't help you, particularly in the murderous part of it." . . .

June 13.—To-day has been appointed a Fast Day. I spent the morning writing a letter on which I put my first Confederate postage-stamp. It is of a brown color and has a large 5 in the center. To-morrow must be devoted to all my foreign correspondents before the expected blockade cuts us off.

June 29.—I attended a fine luncheon yesterday at one of the public schools. A lady remarked to a school official that the cost of provisions in the Confederacy was getting very high, butter, especially, being scarce and costly. "Never fear, my dear madam," he replied. "Texas alone can furnish butter enough to supply the whole Confederacy; we'll soon be getting it from there." It's just as well to have this sublime confidence.

July 15.—The quiet of midsummer reigns, but ripples of excitement break around us as the papers tell of skirmishes and attacks here and there in Virginia. "Rich Mountain" and "Carrick's Ford" were the last. "You see," said Mrs. D. at breakfast to-day, "my prophecy is coming true that Virginia will be the seat of war." "Indeed," I burst out, forgetting my resolution not to argue, "you may think yourselves lucky if this war turns out to have any seat in particular."

So far, no one especially connected with me has gone to fight. How glad I am for his mother's sake that Rob's lameness will keep him at home. Mr. F., Mr. S., and Uncle Ralph are beyond the age for active service, and Edith says Mr. D. can't go now. She is very enthusiastic about other people's husbands being enrolled, and regrets that her Alex is not strong enough to defend his country and his rights.

July 22.—What a day! I feel like one who has been out in a high wind, and cannot get my breath. The newsboys are still shouting with their extras, "Battle of Bull's Run! List of the killed! Battle of Manassas! List of the wounded!" Tender-hearted Mrs. F. was sobbing so she could not serve the tea; but nobody cared for tea. "O G.!" she said, "three thousand of our own, dear Southern boys are lying out there." "My dear Fannie, " spoke Mr. F., "they are heroes now. They died in a glorious cause, and it is not in vain. This will end it. The sacrifice had to be made, but those killed have gained immortal names." Then Rob rushed in with a new extra, reading of the spoils captured, and grief was forgotten. Words cannot paint the excitement. Rob capered about and cheered; Edith danced around ringing the dinner-bell and shouting, "Victory!" Mrs. F. waved a small Confederate flag, while she wiped her eyes, and Mr. D. hastened to the piano and in his most brilliant style struck up "Dixie," followed by "My Maryland" and the "Bonnie Blue Flag."

"Do not look so gloomy, G.," whispered Mr. S. "You should be happy to-night; for, as Mr. F. says, now we shall have peace."

"And is that the way you think of the men of your own blood and race?" I replied. But an utter scorn came over me and choked me, and I walked out of the room. What proof is there in this dark hour that they are not right? Only the emphatic answer of my own soul. . . .

IV
A BELEAGUERED CITY

Oct. 22.—When I came to breakfast this morning Rob was capering over another victory—Ball's Bluff. He would read me, "We pitched the Yankees over the bluff," and ask me in the next breath to go to the theater this evening. I turned on the poor fellow. "Don't tell me about your victories. You vowed by all your idols that the blockade would be raised by October 1, and I notice the ships are still serenely anchored below the city."

"G. you are just as pertinacious yourself in championing your opinions. What sustains you when nobody agrees with you?"

Oct. 28.—When I dropped in at Uncle Ralph's last evening to welcome them back, the whole family were busy at a great center-table copying sequestration acts for the Confederate Government. The property of all Northerners and Unionists is to be sequestrated, and Uncle Ralph can hardly get the work done fast enough. My aunt apologized for the rooms looking chilly; she feared to put the carpets down, as the city might be taken and burned by the Federals. "We are living as much packed up as possible. A signal has been agreed upon, and the instant the army approaches we shall be off to the country again."

Great preparations are being made for defense. At several other places where I called the women were almost hysterical. They seemed to look forward to being blown up with shot and shell, finished with cold steel, or whisked off to some Northern prison. . . .

Nov. 10.—Surely this year will ever be memorable to me for its perfection of natural beauty. Never was sunshine such pure gold, or moonlight such transparent silver. The beautiful custom prevalent here of decking the graves with flowers on All Saints' day was well fulfilled, so profuse and rich were the blossoms. On All-hallow eve Mrs. S. and myself visited a large cemetery. The chrysanthemums lay like great masses of snow and flame and gold in every garden we passed, and were piled on every costly tomb and lowly grave. The battle of Manassas robed many of our women in mourning, and some of those who had no graves to deck were weeping silently as they walked through the scented avenues.

A few days ago Mrs. E. arrived here. She is a widow, of Natchez, a friend of Mrs. F.'s, and is traveling home with the dead body of her eldest son, killed at Manassas. She stopped two days waiting for a boat, and begged me to share her room and read her to sleep, saying she could n't be alone since he was killed; she feared her mind would give way. So I read all the comforting chapters to be found till she dropped into forgetfulness, but the recollection of those weeping mothers in the cemetery banished sleep for me. . . .

SOURCE: *Strange True Stories of Louisiana*,
edited by George Washington Cable
(New York, 1889).

FREDERICK DOUGLASS

Black abolitionist Frederick Douglass wrote prolifically about civil rights. In this speech he condemns both North and South for their contributions to the Civil War. Douglass identifies slavery as the sole cause of the country's ills and chastises each section for its failure to proclaim this fact.

SUBSTANCE OF A LECTURE

Delivered by Frederick Douglass, at
Zion Church, Sunday, June 30.

. . . The present difficulties of our country have brought into notice, far more vividly than ever before, the fact that no nation is absolutely independent of all others. We are not only ruled by national laws, and international laws, but upon all great questions we have to appeal to the great law of the world's public opinion, or the world's judgment. Both the North and the South have been anxious to secure a favorable judgment for themselves in the present contest. We have watched eagerly to see what the London *Times* had to say—what Lord JOHN RUSSELL had to say—and what LOUIS NAPOLEON had to say. No civilized nation can be totally indifferent to the opinion of the rest of mankind. It is an attribute of man's nature to wish to stand approved in the eyes of his fellows; and as of individual men, so of nations. It is impossible to over estimate the self-executing power of this unwritten, but all-pervading law. The settled judgment of mankind, in respect to the right or wrong of any given case, almost shuts the door to argument and doubt. The mightiest of monarchs and the greatest generals have trembled before the verdict of the world. The printing press and the lightning are the most potent rulers of our times. Regiments, battalions, and vast accumulations of munitions of war, are often rendered powerless in the face of the silent moral influence of the world's public opinion.

No people on the globe have ever appealed more emphatically to this tribunal, than have the American people; and yet few people could do so with less success in attaining a desirable verdict. How do we stand now before the bar of the world's opinion? It certainly is a very remarkable fact, and suggestive of the very small influence exerted by particular forms of government, that while Russia, an autocratic Government, is emancipating its serfs, the United States, a democratic Government, is the scene of a bloody civil war for the extension of slavery. The haughty pride of our American civilization may well hang its head and blush at the contrast. It would be a relief to our national self-complacency if the war now going on were really a war between liberty and slavery—if it were abolition on the one hand, and preservation on the other. Such a contest, waged with spirit and determination by the Government against the slaveholding traitors and rebels, would instantly command the respect and sympathy of the civilized world; but, unfortunately, up to the present hour we are entangled with relatives. The South only is positive and absolute. The North is comparative, and, therefore, it is firm in nothing.

Our newspapers and public men express surprise and indignation that European governments have manifested so little sympathy with the Government in suppressing the slaveholding rebels. They have little cause, in my opinion, for this surprise and this indignation. We have ourselves to thank for the chilling blasts that come to us upon every breeze from the Eastern world. We are lukewarm, cursed with halfness, neither hot nor cold. Let but the Government of the U.S. plant itself upon the immutable truth proclaimed in its own Declaration of Independence, that all men are entitled to life, liberty, and the pursuit of happiness, and unsheathe the sword to make this truth the law of the land to all its inhabitants, and it will then deserve, and will receive the cordial and earnest sympathy of the lovers of liberty throughout the world. . . .

I have little admiration for slaveholders in any circumstances; and yet I must accord to them the merit of entire frankness and consistency. They have plunged the country into all the horrors, desolations and abominations of civil war. But they are consistent. They had declared their purpose; they have written piracy and robbery upon every fold of the Confederate flag, and displayed the death head and cross-bones in ghastly horror from the mast heads of their pirate ships.—No one is at a loss to know what they mean. They hate liberty, and say so. They are for slavery, and for all its kindred abominations. Their cause is openly espoused and shamelessly avowed. Ten thousand times over, give me such an enemy, rather than a half-hearted, luke-warm and halting friend!

The anti-slavery cause has, from the beginning, suffered more from the compromising and temporising spirit of the politicians who have undertaken to serve it, than from the assaults of its open and undisguised enemies.—It has often been more injured by the 'ifs' and 'buts' of the politicians, than by the brickbats and unsalable eggs of the pro-slavery mob.

We have now had this war with slaveholders on our hands nearly six months. As yet, no great battle has been fought, and no great victory has been won on either side. Much damage, to be sure, and destruction has taken place. Business has been destroyed, the glory of the country tarnished, doubt and anxiety spread over the land. The forces of the two contending powers have been face to face for weeks and months. Annoying and menacing movements, marches and counter-marches, a battery occasionally attacked, a railway train fired into, a picket shot down by an assassin, a bridge blown up, a house burnt down, a few rebels quickly arrested and as quickly released, thus far make up the incidents of the war. And yet, in this unfinished and almost unbegun state of the conflict of arms, while earnest men in every land are looking for a decision which shall be one thing or the other, and set at rest forever the question whether we, the American people have a Government or not—whether a State has a right to secede—whether a part is more than the whole—whether liberty or slavery shall give law to the Republic, to the shame and confusion of all beholders—the mixed and ill-assorted head, part iron and part clay, of Compromise looms above the sea of our National troubles. Where, under the whole heavens, among what people but the American people could there be, in such a state of facts, even a possibility of compromise? How shall we account for it, even among ourselves? I will tell you. American society, American religion, American government, and every department of American life since the formation of the present Government, with freedom in one section, and slavery in the other, have naturally parted with their native vigor and purity, and degenerated into a compromise, so that an American wherever met with is simply a bundle of contradictions, incongruities and absurdities. For every truth he utters, he has a qualification, and for every principle he lays down, he has an exception. All his doctrines are accompanied with 'ifs' and 'buts.' The attempt to reconcile slavery with freedom has dethroned our logic and converted our statesmanship into stultified imbecility. It has given three tongues to all our politicians, a tongue for the North and a tongue for the South, and a double tongue for the nation.

. . . Thus far our Government has done nothing against the alleged compromises of the Constitution of the United States, the old bond of Union. It has taken up no hostile attitude against slavery itself, and thus has left the door of compromise wide open. This fact, and the additional fact that there are political schemers who still look southward for political support in high and influential positions, increases my apprehension of danger. Until slavery is openly attacked, this danger will continue imminent.

The great and grand mistake of the conduct of the war thus far, is the attitude of our army and Government towards slavery. That attitude deprives us of the moral support of the world. It degrades the war into a war of sections, and robs it of the dignity of being a mighty effort of a great people to vanquish and destroy a huge system of cruelty and barbarism. It gives to the contest the appearance of a struggle for power, rather than a struggle for the advancement and disenthrallment of a nation. It cools the ardor of our troops, and disappoints the hopes of the friends of humanity.

Now, evade and equivocate as we may, slavery is not only the cause of the beginning of this war, but slavery is the sole support of the rebel cause. It is, so to speak, the very stomach of this rebellion.

The war is called a sectional war; but there is nothing in the sections, in the difference of climate or soil to produce conflicts between the two sections. It is not a quarrel between cotton and corn—between live oak and live stock. The two sections are inhabited by the same people. They speak the same language, and are naturally united. There is nothing existing between them to prevent national concord and enjoyment of the profoundest peace, but the existence of slavery. That is the fly in our pot of ointment—the disturbing force in our social system. Every body knows this, every body feels this, and yet the great mass of the people refuse to confess it, and the Government refuses to recognise it.—We talk [of] the irrepressible conflict, and practically give the lie to our talk. We wage war against slaveholding rebels, and yet protect and augment the motive which has moved the slaveholders to rebellion. We strike at the effect, and leave the cause unharmed. Fire will not burn it out of us—water cannot wash it out of us, that this war with the slaveholders can never be brought to a desirable termination until slavery, the guilty cause of all our national troubles, has been totally and forever abolished.

SOURCE: *Douglass' Monthly*
(August 1861).

THE REVEREND JOHN F. W. WARE

A northern Unitarian minister, John F. W. Ware, believes that the initial Union loss on the battlefield at Bull Run is God's punishment for the North's nurturing of the institution of slavery. It was, for instance, mainly New England sea captains who bought and brought Africans to the United States. Ware effectively balances on the shoulders of both North and South the responsibility for slavery and the Civil War.

OUR DUTY UNDER REVERSE

A Sermon Preached in the Church of the "Cambridgeport Parish"
Sunday, 28 July, 1861

. . . I look at this crisis in the national history as one of the judgment-days of God. It is not we who have been outraged by the South,—we who are to punish; but we have ourselves been false to God, and are under chastisement. North, as well as South, has sinned, and come far short of what it was her duty to do. I wish we could look at it that way. Men who live and believe only in to-day—who have never watched God in history—have no idea of his sure retributions; how clearly can be traced his visitings upon national dereliction and crime. History is largely only retribution; the generation possibly escaping, but the iniquity visited on the third and fourth unerringly. One who knows all that, must feel that we are under the divine displeasure, and that because of our infidelity to our privilege and our profession is this terrible scourge upon us. A little and loyal one, planted here in the wilderness, became a thousand. God nourished the vine the fathers planted. We grew to a great people. We stood before kings. There was none superior. On the sea, on the land, we knew no masters; and the sun, in all his course, saw no land blessed like this. But our nation was builded upon a principle. It had a base such as none other. Not the mere accident of discovery, the necessity of migration, the freak of traffic, a better climate, or the lure of gold, made it; but a broad, eternal truth, which nations had sighed and groped after,—which sighing and groping nations ever since have recognized as the one great thing needed to their healing. That is the source of our prosperity, that had made us a name to be trembled at and revered,—that gave us the grasp we had,—was the single secret of our success. But it entailed duties upon us, to which, it is proved, we were not equal. We struck the parricidal blow when at the height of our prosperity. The principle on which our fathers builded was stigmatized as a "sounding and glittering generality." Men who held to the old faith of the founders were taunted about a "higher law." Slavery, in the early day, the small cloud of evil, in ours had swelled to the gigantic, overmastering tyranny; ever more and more imperious, getting, only to cry "more." Nothing it asked for but it had. Compromise sapped the manhood, the integrity, of the North. Trade, manufactures, social position, expediency, party policy, fiercely seconded the most exorbitant demand. Slavery became national; and, before the slavepower, this fair, vast heritage, sacred to freedom, trembled, yielded, and was all but lost.

Now, it is impossible that such desertion of principle, such timid yielding, should go unpunished. We had basely surrendered that which came to us consecrated by the trials, tears, prayers, blood, of our ancestors. We had the advance post in the great cause of civilization and Christianity, and we fled from it in base and causeless panic. We talked of freedom; our boast was, that the humblest, seeking the protection of our flag, was safe: while we gave the lie to all, not by the existence of slavery, which we could not help; not by its horrors, which we could not control; but by fawning before its power, helping it to any thing it desired. Esau sold his birthright when he was starving; and the name of that poor, starving man has gone to the ages in undeserved opprobrium. We bartered ours when we were full, and that we might hold to our trade and our manufactures, our comfort and our gold,— to peace, though bought at the price of disgrace,—consented to yield our trust. It is the blackest blot on the record of human history. If the act of starving Esau have covered his memory with shame, what shall the coming ages have in store for this generation?

Shall God stand by, and not avenge himself? It is come: "*Mene, mene, tekel, upharsin.*" The great laws of God override our human policies, and vindicate themselves in our disasters. Our trade, our commerce, our plenty, our peace,—where are they? What has the cringing and fawning and compromising, and denial of principle and manhood, yielded? To-day the cry of battle is in the land; to-day the prestige of our old fame is gone; to-day enterprise stands dumb, the wheels of industry are idle, the white sails furled; all is disorganized: and, if we look about us for the cause, it is that we have sinned.

. . . I believe myself a patriot. I believe this nation set among the peoples to work out a great problem. I believe her sun will never set, till her sounding and glittering generalities, her mere abstractions, shall have become the solid corner in the foundation of all realms. . . .

There is no room in the present for doubt or fear. Every thing encourages. It is a vast stride the cause has taken since last Sunday's bloody field. What victory could have done the like? Already God's hand is seen in the reverse. It was needed: it is working well. May it work completely!—purging away all low motive; cleansing our coun-

cils of all but patriotism and faith, our armies of all but courage and
honor, ourselves of all but conviction of the holiness of our cause, and
confidence in God. Let the army and the people, the rulers and the
ruled, now advance in sympathy and mutual respect. Let there be no
chicane, no meddling, no hypercriticism. Let ours be union indeed:
and then again, speedily, the holy banner of freedom—the well-loved,
well-tried "stars and stripes"—shall spring to its place in the clear
upper air; and, as its graceful folds unbend themselves to the woo-
ing of every wind, the nations shall look up to see in it the assurance
that every chain is snapped, and there is on earth, not only peace, but
LIBERTY!

SOURCE: *Our Duty Under Reverse: A Sermon Preached
in the Church of the Cambridgeport Parish*
(Boston, 1861).

WALT WHITMAN

When the Civil War started, Walt Whitman began Drum-
Taps, *a volume of war poems. In two selections here, the
sensitive Unionist writer captures the contrary moods of
that first year and its displacement of all social organiza-
tions, occupations, domestic relationships, and even the
dead.*

EIGHTEEN SIXTY-ONE

ARM'D year—year of the struggle,
No dainty rhymes or sentimental love verses for you terrible year,
Not you as some pale poetling seated at a desk lisping cadenzas
        piano,
But as a strong man, erect, clothed in blue clothes, advancing,
        carrying a rifle on your shoulder,
With well-gristled body and sunburnt face and hands, with a knife
        in the belt at your side,
As I heard you shouting loud, your sonorous voice ringing across
        the continent,
Your masculine voice O year, as rising amid the great cities,
Amid the men of Manhattan I saw you as one of the workmen,
        the dwellers in Manhattan,
Or with large steps crossing the prairies out of Illinois and
        Indiana,
Rapidly crossing the West with springy gait and descending the
        Alleghanies,
Or down from the great lakes or in Pennsylvania, or on deck
        along the Ohio river;

Or southward along the Tennessee or Cumberland rivers, or at
     Chattanooga on the mountain top,
Saw I your gait and saw I your sinewy limbs clothed in blue,
     bearing weapons, robust year,
Heard your determin'd voice launch'd forth again and again,
Year that suddenly sang by the mouths of the round lipp'd cannon,
I repeat you, hurrying, crashing, sad, distracted year.

BEAT! BEAT! DRUMS!

BEAT! beat! drums!—blow! bugles! blow!
Through the windows—through doors—burst like a ruthless
     force,
Into the solemn church, and scatter the congregation,
Into the school where the scholar is studying;
Leave not the bridegroom quiet—no happiness must he have
     now with his bride,
Nor the peaceful farmer any peace, ploughing his field or gathering
     his grain,
So fierce you whirr and pound you drums—so shrill you bugles
     blow.

Beat! beat! drums!—blow! bugles! blow!
Over the traffic of cities—over the rumble of wheels in the streets;
Are beds prepared for sleepers at night in the houses? no sleepers
     must sleep in those beds,
No bargainers' bargains by day—no brokers or speculators—
     would they continue?
Would the talkers be talking? would the singer attempt to sing?
Would the lawyer rise in the court to state his case before the
     judge?
Then rattle quicker, heavier drums—you bugles wilder blow.

Beat! beat! drums!—blow! bugles! blow!
Make no parley—stop for no expostulation,
Mind not the timid—mind not the weeper or prayer,
Mind not the old man beseeching the young man,
Let not the child's voice be heard, nor the mother's entreaties,
Make even the trestles to shake the dead where they lie awaiting
     the hearses,
So strong you thump O terrible drums—so loud you bugles blow.

SOURCE: *Leaves of Grass*
(Philadelphia, 1883).

CHARLES MINOR BLACKFORD

Charles Minor Blackford, a Virginia lawyer and the father of three children, was twenty-seven when he joined the Confederate army as a lieutenant. During the next four years he advanced to the rank of major, serving mainly in Virginia but also as far north as Gettysburg and as far south as Georgia. Throughout the war he wrote long letters to his wife, demonstrating an artist's eye for closely observed detail.

LETTER

July 20, 1861 . . . Just as we crossed Bull Run I saw Edmund Fontaine, . . . of Hanover, resting on a log on the roadside. I asked him what was the matter, and he said he was wounded and was dying. He said it very cheerfully and did not look as if anything was the matter, but as we came back we found him dead and some of his comrades about to remove his body. It was a great shock to me, as I had known him from his boyhood. . . .

That was a day long to be remembered, and such a Sunday as men seldom spend. To all but a scattered few it was our first battle, and its sights and wonders were things of which we had read but scarcely believed or understood until seen and experienced. The rout of the enemy was complete, but our generals showed much want of skill in not making the material advantages greater. The Federal army was equipped with every species of munition and property, while ours was wanting in everything. They were stricken with a panic, and wherever the panic was increased by the sight of an armed rebel it discovered itself by the natural impulse to throw away arms and accoutrements and to abandon everything in the shape of cannon, caissons, wagons, ambulances and provisions which might impede their flight, yet they managed, despite their precipitate flight, to carry off much. They lost only some thirty-odd cannon, for example, while with proper management on our part they would not have reached the Potomac with two whole batteries, and so with the other properties. . . .

During the evening as I was riding over part of the field where there were many dead yankees lying who had been killed, . . . I noticed an old doll-baby with only one leg lying by the side of a Federal soldier just as it dropped out of his pocket when he fell writhing in the agony of death. It was obviously a memento of some little loved one at home which he had brought so far with him and had worn close to his heart on this day of danger and death. It was strange to see that emblem of childhood, that token of a father's love, lying there amidst the dead and dying where the storm of war had so fiercely raged and where death had stalked in the might of its terrible majesty. I dismounted, picked it up and stuffed it back into the poor fellow's cold bosom, that it might rest with him in the bloody grave which was to be forever unknown to those who loved and mourned him in his distant home.

The actual loss of the enemy I do not know, but their dead extended for miles and their wounded filled every house and shed in the neighborhood. The wounded doubtless suffered much. Their own surgeons abandoned their field hospitals and joined the fleeing cohorts of the living, and our surgeons had all they could do to look after our own wounded, who of course were first served. They received kind treatment, however, and as soon as our surgeons were free they rendered all the aid in their power.

. . . Along the road and in the midst of abandoned cannon and wagons we found many a forsaken carriage and hack with half-eaten lunches and half-used baskets of champagne, and we received most laughable accounts from the citizens on the roadside of the scenes they saw and the sharp contrast between the proud and confident advance and the wild panic of the flight. The men of our company got many articles of spoil not known to the ordnance department or used by the *men* who fill the ranks of war. . . .

Source: *Memoirs of Life In and Out of the Army in
Virginia During the War Between the States*
(Lynchburg, Va., 1894–96).

SULLIVAN BALLOU

*During the first summer of the war Sullivan Ballou, a
Union soldier from Rhode Island, articulated the moral
and psychological dilemma of the Civil War volunteer.
His anxiety over leaving his wife and two sons gave way
to satisfaction with his decision and his acceptance of the
possibility of death. The first letter is to a friend, and the
last two are addressed to his wife. The final missive, an
eloquent love letter, expresses Ballou's passion for both
wife and country. Here the mystery at the heart of warfare, how a person can sacrifice all that he holds most
dear for the sake of a national cause, is made clear.*

LETTER TO A FRIEND

Providence June 11 1861

My very dear friend

Governor Sprague has tendered me the Commission of Major in the 2nd Regiment of R.I. Detached Militia and I have accepted it. In the hasty and somewhat confused contemplation of my new position which I have been able to give it, my heart yearns for friendly converse with you. You have long been too kind to me—and I have too long resorted to you for encouragement and advice not to think of you now when I realize the full value of all my friends and the pain and loss of parting from them. God bless you and reward you as the truest friend I ever had.

I have searched my conduct and motives to know if I have done wrong in thus changing and perhaps periling the course of my life, and I am not sensible of having wronged myself or my family; but the bare thought of leaving my wife and little boys is full of intense pain. It was one thing to talk over the matter before I accepted the commission and a very different thing to feel that I am now under marching orders. If I fall I know it can never be in a better cause. I am too thoroughly convinced of the justice of this war—know too well the peril of our free institutions and the value to the world of our American civilization, even to hesitate to cast in my life if it is called for; but I have felt too keenly the sufferings and pangs of orphanhood and have seen too many trials of the widowed mother not to fear for my dear little boys and tremble for my wife. If necessary will you not sometime give them that kind and effective counsel you have often given me.

Do not think me weak or lacking in courage in thus expressing the only feeling that burdens my heart. I could not help doing it to you.

I shall doubtless see you before we leave, as I must come to town and arrange a few little matters I have there. Can you not induce Smith to pay that draft before I go; He is not aware how much I need that money, or he would pay it promptly.

Yours affectionately
S. Ballou.

LETTERS TO SARAH

Camp Sprague [Washington, D.C.]
Sunday June 23rd / 61

My dear Sarah,

I wrote to you very hurriedly & confusedly yesterday soon after our arrival; and feel again as tho I wanted to write you a little more. We are encamped in Paradise. There certainly never was a more beautiful spot. It is an oak grove—the trees all tall and large and the ground free from shrubs. The space we occupy is about half the size of the camp at home and while the sun is pouring down its oppressive heat out side, we are as cool and comfortable as you could wish. While the first regiment is encamped close beside us in booths or sheds and rather cramped for room and oftentimes go outside on the ground to sleep, we are all cool and our white tents in the green woods look more inviting than anything else. Our baggage waggons stand close behind *our* row of tents—one just at the back door of my tent to which my good horse "Jennie" is tied night & day. My man* sleeps in the baggage waggon and I occupy my tent alone much to my delight—he is a kind good natured fellow & I like him much. He now begins to understand his duties & will fill them I have no doubt. Last night I slept in my tent for the first time, & I slept well: have not caught cold and my catarrh continues better. Last night the moon was full I believe & if you could have seen it shining through our trees & glistening on our white tents you would have said it was the most beautiful sight you ever saw. When I went to bed I lay a long time looking up to see the shadows of the leaves and branches painted on my tent & at last went to sleep thinking of my loved wife & my little boys. This morning Bishop Clarke preached to us about half an hour, and spoke with his usual force & eloquence. . . . We are about two miles from Washington; & from the hill where the first Regt. are encamped the city & all its buildings can be seen. Tomorrow afternoon at 3 P.M. we are to march down to the White house to be reviewed by the President & Gen. Scott. What is to be done with us I know not. . . .

The first regiment are in splendid health—they are brown and stout as you can imagine. On their return from Harpers ferry they marched 32 miles in 17 hours & feel very proud of it. Our Regiment are all well—among the whole 1000 there is scarcely an ail. You need not think I have put a shining face on, to cheer you up; I really have not exagerated our agreeable situation. At the same time do not harbor the thought that I fail to think of my loved ones at home—they are always in my heart and scarcely ever absent from my mind. I have just begun to realize that though I am here with 2000 men I am yet alone. I am far away from you Sarah & my beautiful boys—and it seems strange to me that I have never prized you as I ought—however much I may have loved you. I yearn to see you now so much, when I know I cannot, that all the love I have heretofore poured out for you seems insignificant. When I could go home every day & see you all, I did not think to weigh you in the scales with my affection; but now I think day by day what a trio I have, far away in my home.

When shall I hear from you: perhaps you are writing me today. I hope so—& that you will write me long letters full of all the little incidents of your daily life & that of the children. Be of good cheer & bear

---

*Ballou's servant

our present separation like the noble christian woman that you are. I already look forward to the time when I shall come home to you safe & well & I pray God I may find you & my dear children all well & rejoiced to see me. I wish you would go out & see my mother often & comfort her. I cannot write her many letters unless I lessen the number to you—& that I do not wish to do—so you must see her and tell her all the news from me. You must not wait for letters from me, dear Sarah but write me as often as you can find a few moments to spare for I shall look for your letters *now* with as much impatience as I used to when a lover's ardor fired me almost to desperation.

. . . There is a rumor to night that the rebels will attack our lines on Arlington Heights to *night* & that the 1st Regiment has marching orders—but there are so many rumors of the same kind that nobody takes any notice of it. I doubt the rumor & rather believe that there will be no general battle for some time. It will be very unwise to put *our* regiment into the field on account of our bad arms. We shall probably be furnished with rifles & we must be drilled with them some time before the men can use them well. . . .

. . . Goodbye my dear Sarah
& believe me

Yours affectionately
Sullivan.

The Adjutant here is a fine flute player & has his flute with him & good music. When you learn of some one coming *directly here* send my Ivory topped flute by him.

July 14th 1861
Camp Clark Washington

My very dear Sarah

The indications are very strong that we shall move in a few days—perhaps tomorrow. Lest I should not be able to write to you again, I feel impelled to write a few lines that may fall under your eye when I shall be no more. Our movement may be one of a few days duration and full of pleasure, and it may be one of severe conflict and death to me. "Not my will, but thine O God be done." If it is necessary that I should fall on the battle field for my country, I am ready. I have no misgivings about, or lack of confidence in the cause in which I am engaged, & my courage does not halt or falter. I know how strongly American civilization now leans on the triumph of the government, &

how great a debt we owe to those who went before us through the blood and sufferings of the Revolution, & I am willing, perfectly willing—to lay down all my joys in this life to help maintain this government & to pay that debt. But, my dear wife, when I know that with my own joys, I lay down nearly all of yours, & replace them in this life with cares & sorrows, when after having eaten for long years the bitter fruits of orphanage my self, I must offer it as the only sustenance to my dear little children, is it mean or dishonorable that while the banner of my purpose floats calmly & proudly in the breeze, underneath, my unbounded love for you, my darling wife & children should struggle in fierce, though useless contest with my love of Country. I cannot describe to you my feelings on this calm summer Sabbath night, when thousands now are sleeping around me, many of them enjoying, perhaps the last sleep before that of death, while I am suspicious that death is creeping around me with his fatal dart, as I sit communing with God, my country and thee. I have sought most closely and diligently & often in my heart for a wrong motive in thus hazarding the happiness of all those I love and I could find none. A pure love of my country and of the principles I have so often advocated before the people. Another name of honor that I love more than I fear death, has called upon me, & I have obeyed.

Sarah, my love for you is deathless: it seems to bind me with mighty cables that nothing but misfortune could break; and yet my love of Country comes over me like a strong wind & bears me irresistibly on with all those charms to the battle field. The memories of all the blissful moments I have spent with you come creeping over me, & I feel most grateful to God & to you that I have enjoyed them so long, and how hard it is for me to give them up & burn to ashes the hopes of future years. Where God willing, we might still have lived and loved together, & seen our sons grown up to honorable manhood around us. I have, I know but few & small claims upon Divine Providence—but something whispers to me perhaps it is the wafted prayer of my little Edgar, that I shall return to my loved ones unharmed. If I do not, my dear Sarah never forget how much I loved you, and when my last breath escapes me—on the battle field—it will whisper your name. Forgive my many faults, and the many pains I have caused you. How thoughtless how foolish I have oftentimes been. How gladly would I wash out with my tears every little spot upon your happiness, & struggle with all the misfortunes of this world to shield you & your children from harm. But I cannot. I must watch you from the spirit land, and hover near you—while you buffet the storms with your precious freight, and wait with patience till we meet to part no more. But, O Sarah! if the dead can come back to this earth & flit unseen around those they loved, I shall always be near you. In the gladdest days, & in the darkest night, amidst your happiest scenes, and gloomiest hours, always—*always*, and if there be a soft breeze upon your cheek it shall be my breath; or the cool air fans your throbbing temples; it shall be my spirit passing by.

Sarah, do not mourn me dead, think I am gone and wait for thee, for we shall meet again. As for my little boys—they will grow up as I have done, and never know a father's love or care. Little Willie is too young to remember me long—and my blue-eyed Edgar—will keep my frolics with him among the dim memories of his childhood.

Sarah, I have unbounded confidence in your maternal care, & your development of their characters, and feel that God will bless you in your holy work. Tell my two mothers I call God's blessing upon them. O Sarah; come to me, and lead thither my children.

Sullivan

SOURCE: Ballou Correspondence,
Rhode Island Historical Society Library, mss. 277.

SECTION 2 1862

At the beginning of 1862 most northerners were optimistic that the war would be brief. President Lincoln never recognized the Confederate states as a separate nation, but rather viewed their secession as an insurrection. He hoped that a blockade of ports and an infiltration of federal troops throughout the South, especially around Richmond, Virginia, the Confederate capital, would pressure the southern states back into the Union. But when Confederate forces scored victories in the Seven Days' battles, the battle of Shiloh, and the Second Battle of Bull Run, Lincoln and the North recognized that reuniting the country would take more than a limited military engagement.

By mid-1862 it could no longer be denied that for the North slavery had become the foremost issue of the Civil War. By this time, Congress had already abolished slavery in Washington, D.C., decreed that army officers could no longer return fugitive slaves to their masters, and offered compensation to slave owners who voluntarily freed their slaves. In July, Congress granted Lincoln the authority to enlist blacks into military service, and by September President Lincoln had drafted a preliminary Emancipation Proclamation. He needed a Union victory, however, in order to issue it. One near victory came on September 17 in the Battle of Antietam or, as the Confederate forces called it, the Battle of Sharpsburg. While federal forces prevented southern troops from advancing farther into Maryland, the brutality and loss of lives in America's bloodiest day of fighting thus far sobered fighters on both sides.

Although the Confederacy had the advantage of fighting the war on familiar territory, it was not without severe problems. Rations and inflation began to depress the morale of southern soldiers and civilians. And the southern states resented President of the Confederate States of America Jefferson Davis's call for troops and supplies, viewing conscription as a central government's interference in their rights. By late 1862 doubts about the feasibility of individual sovereign states were beginning to grow.

These readings demonstrate the country's recognition that the end of the war had receded from view and that fear, loss, poverty, and injustice would persist as well.

FREDERICK DOUGLASS

In this speech delivered in Philadelphia, black abolition-ist Frederick Douglass again makes the call he has been repeating since the start of the war, that black men be allowed by the United States government to enlist in the Union forces. To persuade his audience, he invokes history, religion, military strategy, and the philosophical concept of the free and equal human being embedded in the Declaration of Independence. Because so many white northerners resist such arguments from Douglass and other abolitionists, the debate continues.

SPEECH OF FREDERICK DOUGLASS ON THE WAR

Delivered in National Hall, Philadelphia
JANUARY 14, 1862

. . . But how shall the rebellion be put down? I will tell you; but be-fore I do so, you must allow me to say that the plan thus far pursued does not correspond with my humble notion of fitness. Thus far, it must be confessed, we have struck wide of the mark, and very feebly withal. The temper of our steel has proved much better than the tem-per of our minds. While I do not charge, as some have done, that the Government at Washington is conducting the war upon peace princi-ples, it is very plain that the war is *not* being conducted on war prin-ciples.

We are fighting the rebels with only one hand, when we ought to be fighting them with both. We are recruiting our troops in the towns and villages of the North, when we ought to be recruiting them on the plantations of the South. We are striking the guilty rebels with our soft, white hand, when we should be striking with the iron hand of the black man, which we keep chained behind us. We have been catching slaves, instead of arming them. We have thus far repelled our natural friends to win the worthless and faithless friendship of our unnatural enemies. We have been endeavoring to heal over the rotten cancer of slavery, instead of cutting out its death-dealing roots and fibres. We pay more attention to the advice of the half-rebel State of Kentucky, than to any suggestion coming from the loyal North. We have shouldered all the burdens of slavery, and given the slaveholders and traitors all its benefits; and robbed our cause of half its dignity in the eyes of an on-looking world. . . .

I have been often asked since this war began, why I am not at the South battling for freedom. My answer is with the Government. The Washington Government wants men for its army, but thus far, it has not had the boldness to recognize the manhood of the race to which I belong. It only sees in the slave an article of commerce—a contraband. I do not wish to say aught against our Government, for good or bad; it is all we have to save us from anarchy and ruin; but I owe it to my race, in view of the cruel aspersions cast upon it, to affirm that, in denying them the privileges to fight for their country, they have been most deeply and grievously wronged. Neither in the Revolution, nor in the last war did any such narrow and contemptible policy obtain. It shows the deep degeneracy of our times—the height from which we have fallen—that, while Washington, in 1776, and Jackson, in 1814, could fight side by side with negroes, now, not even the best of our generals are willing so to fight. Is McClellan better than Washington? Is Halleck better than Jackson?

One situation only has been offered me, and that is the office of a body servant to a Colonel. I would not despise even that, if I could by accepting it be of service to my enslaved fellow-countrymen. In the temple of impartial liberty there is no seat too low for me. But one thing I have a right to ask when I am required to endure the hardships and brave the dangers of the battle field. I ask that I shall have either a country, or the hope of a country under me—a Government, or the hope of a Government around me, and a flag of impartial liberty floating over me.

We have recently had a solemn fast, and have offered up innumerable prayers for the deliverance of the nation from its manifold perils and calamities. I say nothing against these prayers. Their subjective power is indispensable; but I know also, that the work of making, and the work of answering them, must be performed by the same hands. If the loyal North shall succeed in suppressing this foul and scandalous rebellion, that achievement will be due to the amount of wisdom and force they bring against the rebels in arms.

Thus far we have shown no lack of force. A call for men is answered by half a million. A call for money brings down a hundred million. A call for prayers brings a nation to its altars. But still the rebellion rages.—Washington is menaced. The Potomac is blockaded.

Jeff. Davis is still proud and defiant, and the rebels are looking forward hopefully to a recognition of their independence, the breaking of the blockade, and their final severance from the North.

Now, what is the remedy for all this? The answer is ready. Have done at once and forever with the wild and guilty phantasy that any one man can have a right of property in the body and soul of another man. Have done with the now exploded idea that the old Union, which has hobbled along through seventy years upon the crutches of compromise, is either desirable or possible, now, or in the future. Accept the incontestible truth of the "irrepressible conflict." It was spoken when temptations to compromise were less strong than now. Banish from your political dreams the last lingering adumbration that this great American nation can ever rest firmly and securely upon a mixed basis, part of iron, part of clay, part free and part slave. The experiment has been tried, and tried, too, under more favorable circumstances than any which the future is likely to offer, and has deplorably failed. Now lay the axe at the root of the tree, and give it—root, top, body and branches—to the consuming fire.—You have now the opportunity. . . .

SOURCE: *Douglass' Monthly*
(February 1862).

JOHN GILBERT

One of the few Union strongholds in the South by early 1862 was a section of the coast of South Carolina. John Gilbert, a member of the Third Regiment of New Hampshire Volunteers, reveals another hardship of war, that of the soldier's family deprived now of his previous income. Some states, like New Hampshire, required their towns to pay $12 a month to enlisted men's families but the municipalities did not always meet their obligations.

LETTER TO A FRIEND

Port Royal, Hilton Head
South Carolina
Feb. 4th 1862

Dear Sir: I thought I would write you a few lines knowing that you are the only friend to me and my family. I take this privilege in addressing myself to you although I have no right to do so. My family are suffering by all accounts I can hear through the neglect of the select men of the town of Cornish they take the advantage of my wife because I suppose she is a woman they deny her the pay which the State of New Hampshire is bound by law to pay her every town in the State of N.H. pays the Soldiers families their honest dues whatever in fact the law allows them It appears to me there must be a many ignorant men in the town of Cornish or else they want to cheat my wife out of her rights and what is justly due to her Perhaps they may have the Idea that the money comes out of their own town but it comes out of the State as well as the town. My wife tells me in her last letter that they deal with her as if she was a pauper and on the town which is absolutely wrong, by giving her a little flour once in while and a little wood nows and thens perhaps they think they will get out of it by dealing with her in this kind of manner but I tell you Sir they will have to pay her the 12 Dollars per month which the law specifies she shall have as a Soldiers Wife this will be seen to if I get home once again for the town of Cornish shall be answerable for that amount of money. I wish my dear friend if it would lay in your power to help her to get her money that you will do all you can towards it out of kindness to me and compassion to my family, . . .

J. Gilbert

SOURCE: Letters of John Gilbert, New Hampshire
Historical Society, mss. 1900–001.

SARAH MORGAN DAWSON

By mid-1862 federal forces controlled most of the Mississippi River, preventing the export of cotton and the import of military and civilian goods and crippling the southern economy. Sarah Morgan Dawson, a young southern woman, writes in her diary about the upheaval, confusion, and insecurity she and her family face living in New Orleans under Union occupation.

APRIL 26TH, 1862

There is no word in the English language that can express the state in which we are, and have been, these last three days. Day before yesterday, news came early in the morning of three of the enemy's boats passing the Forts, and then the excitement began. It increased rapidly on hearing of the sinking of eight of our gunboats in the engagement, the capture of the Forts, and last night, of the burning of the wharves and cotton in the city* while the Yankees were taking possession. To-day, the excitement has reached the point of delirium. I believe I am one of the most self-possessed in my small circle; and yet I feel such a craving for news of Miriam, and mother, and Jimmy, who are in the city, that I suppose I am as wild as the rest. It is nonsense to tell me I am cool, with all these patriotic and enthusiastic sentiments. Nothing can be positively ascertained, save that our gunboats are sunk, and theirs are coming up to the city. Everything else has been contradicted until we really do not know whether the city has been taken or not. We only know we had best be prepared for anything. So day before yesterday, Lilly and I sewed up our jewelry, which may be of use if we have to fly. I vow I will not move one step, unless carried away. Come what will, here I remain.

We went this morning to see the cotton burning—a sight never before witnessed, and probably never again to be seen. Wagons, drays,—everything that can be driven or rolled,—were loaded with the bales and taken a few squares back to burn on the commons. Negroes were running around, cutting them open, piling them up, and setting them afire. All were as busy as though their salvation depended on disappointing the Yankees. Later, Charlie sent for us to come to the river and see him fire a flatboat loaded with the precious material for which the Yankees are risking their bodies and souls. Up and down the levee, as far as we could see, negroes were rolling it down to the brink of the river where they would set them afire and push the bales in to float burning down the tide. Each sent up its wreath of smoke and looked like a tiny steamer puffing away. Only I doubt that from the source to the mouth of the river there are as many boats afloat on the Mississippi. The flatboat was piled with as many bales as it could hold without sinking. Most of them were cut open, while negroes staved in the heads of barrels of alcohol, whiskey, etc., and dashed bucketsful over the cotton. Others built up little chimneys of pine every few feet, lined with pine knots and loose cotton, to burn more quickly. There, piled the length of the whole levee, or burning in the river, lay the work of thousands of negroes for more than a year past. It had come from every side. Men stood by who owned the cotton that was burning or

---

*Southerners burned the mainstay of their economy, cotton, to prevent the North from getting it for their textile mills. The South believed that burning or not harvesting cotton also increased its demand and would entice Great Britain and France to come to their aid.

waiting to burn. They either helped, or looked on cheerfully. Charlie owned but sixteen bales—a matter of some fifteen hundred dollars; but he was the head man of the whole affair, and burned his own, as well as the property of others. A single barrel of the whiskey that was thrown on the cotton, cost the man who gave it one hundred and twenty-five dollars. (It shows what a nation in earnest is capable of doing.) Only two men got on the flatboat with Charlie when it was ready. It was towed to the middle of the river, set afire in every place, and then they jumped into a little skiff fastened in front, and rowed to land. The cotton floated down the Mississippi one sheet of living flame, even in the sunlight. It would have been grand at night. But then we will have fun watching it this evening anyway; for they cannot get through to-day, though no time is to be lost. Hundreds of bales remain untouched. An incredible amount of property has been destroyed to-day; but no one begrudges it. Every grog-shop has been emptied, and gutters and pavements are floating with liquors of all kinds. So that if the Yankees are fond of strong drink, they will fare ill.

Yesterday, Mr. Hutchinson and a Dr. Moffat called to ask for me, with a message about Jimmy. I was absent, but they saw Lilly. Jimmy, they said, was safe. Though sick in bed, he had sprung up and rushed to the wharf at the first tap of the alarm bell in New Orleans. But as nothing could be done, he would probably be with us to-day, bringing mother and Miriam. I have neither heard nor seen more. The McRae, they said, went to the bottom, with the others. They did not know whether any one aboard had escaped. God be praised that Jimmy was not on her then! The new boat to which he was appointed is not yet finished. So he is saved! . . . Mr. Hutchinson was on his way above, going to join others where the final battle is to be fought on the Mississippi. He had not even time to sit down; so I was doubly grateful to him for his kindness. I wish I could have thanked him for being so considerate of me in my distress now. In her agitation, Lilly gave him a letter I had been writing to George when I was called away; and begged him to address it and mail it at Vicksburg, or somewhere; for no mail will leave here for Norfolk for a long while to come. The odd part is, that he does not know George. But he said he would gladly take charge of it and remember the address, which Lilly told him was Richmond. Well! if the Yankees get it they will take it for an insane scrawl. I wanted to calm his anxiety about us, though I was so wildly excited that I could only say, "Don't mind us! We are safe. But fight, George! Fight for us!" The repetition was ludicrous. I meant so much, too! I only wanted him to understand he could best defend us there. Ah! Mr. Yankee! if you had but your brothers in this world, and their lives hanging by a thread, you too might write wild letters! And if you want to know what an excited girl can do, just call and let me show you the use of a small seven-shooter and a large carving-knife which vibrate between my belt and my pocket, always ready for emergencies.

APRIL 27TH

. . . I went to church; but I grew very anxious before it was over, feeling that I was needed at home. When I returned, I found Lilly wild with excitement, picking up hastily whatever came to hand, preparing for instant flight, she knew not where. The Yankees were in sight; the town was to be burned; we were to run to the woods, etc. If the house had to be burned, I had to make up my mind to run, too. So my treasure-bag tied around my waist as a bustle, a sack with a few necessary articles hanging on my arm, some few quite unnecessary ones, too, as I had not the heart to leave the old and new prayer books father had given me, and Miriam's too;—pistol and carving-knife ready, I stood awaiting the exodus. I heaped on the bed the treasures I wanted to burn, matches lying ready to fire the whole at the last minute. I may here say that, when all was over, I found I had omitted many things from the holocaust. This very diary was not included. It would have afforded vast amusement to the Yankees. There may yet be occasion to burn them, and the house also. People fortunately changed their minds about the *auto-da-fé* just then; and the Yankees have not yet arrived, at sundown. So, when the excitement calmed down, poor Lilly tumbled in bed in a high fever in consequence of terror and exertion.

SOURCE: *A Confederate Girl's Diary*
(Boston, 1913).

ISAIAH C. WEARS

One of the options President Lincoln considered was the voluntary relocation of some black Americans to Central America. He gave this rationale for his plan: "your race suffer very greatly, many of them by living among us, while ours suffer from your presence. . . . See our present condition—the country engaged in war! our white men cutting one another's throats. . . . But for your race among us there could not be war. . . ." Isaiah C. Wears, a black abolitionist, defends in this response to the President's proposal the black population's right to remain in the country of their birth and in an African-American culture over two hundred years old.

LINCOLN'S COLONIZATION PROPOSAL IS ANTI-CHRISTIAN

To be asked, after so many years of oppression and wrong have been inflicted in a land and by a people who have been so largely enriched by the black man's toil, to pull up stakes in a civilized and Christian nation and to go to an uncivilized and barbarous nation, simply to gratify an unnatural wicked prejudice emanating from slavery, is unreasonable and anti-Christian in the extreme.

How unaccountably strange it seems, that wise men familiar with the history of this country, with the history of slavery, with the rebellion and its merciless outrages, yet are apparently totally ignorant of the true cause of the war—or, if not ignorant, afraid or ashamed to charge the guilt where it belongs.

Men profess to believe in God and the Bible, justice and humanity, but notwithstanding numerous examples in every age's history vividly showing how cruel has been the oppressor's rule and how invariably his heinous practices have brought on wars and destruction, with God's sore displeasure and heavy judgments—it is easy, nevertheless, to find excuses to ignore truth, to defy God's vengeance and trample on his creatures.

Says the President: The colored race are the cause of the war. So were the children of Israel the cause of the troubles in Egypt. So was Christ the cause of great commotions in Judea, in this same sense; and those identified with Him were considered of the baser sort, and really unfit for citizenship.

But surely the President did not mean to say that our race was the cause of the war, but the occasion thereof.

If black men are here in the way of white men, they did not come here of their own accord. Their presence is traceable to the white man's lust for power, love of oppression and disregard of the plain teachings of the Lord Jesus Christ, whose rule enjoins upon all men to "do unto others as they would be done by." Although a man may have had the misfortune to fall among thieves and become wounded and distressed by the wayside, the great Examplar would not recognize the right of either the Levite or priest to shield themselves behind their prejudices or selfishness and thus leave him to suffer.

But it is not the Negro that is the cause of the war; it is the unwillingness on the part of the American people to do the race simple justice. It is not social equality to be made the equal of the white man, to have kind masters to provide for him, or to find for him congenial homes in Africa or Central America that he needs, but he desires not to be robbed of his labor—to be deprived of his God-given rights.

The effect of this scheme of colonization, we fear, will be to arouse prejudice and to increase enmity against us, without bringing with it the remedy proposed or designed.

Repentance is more needed on the part of our oppressors than anything else. Could a policy that would lead to this wholesome course be adopted, some bright hope might be seen for the triumph of freedom and justice.

If the African race are not of a color most pleasing to their fairer-skinned brother, let the fault be charged upon the Creator, as the same hand that made the white man made the black man also. God has revealed no distinction in His word, touching the color of a man's skin.

But we are to leave this country on the score of selfishness to make room for our selfish white neighbor to sail smoothly, it was intimated.

True, enactments of terrible severity may be passed calculated to ostracize us—it will be strange if the President's suggestions do not directly invite persecutions of an aggravating character. But in our sober reflections, let us remember that Great Britain has got possessions adapted to our people, both of Southern and Northern birth in the Canada, and the West Indies, that are free for all colors—governed by laws that recognize no difference of a complexional character—admit all as equal citizens who will support the government. The humblest fugitive slave as well as those of noblest blood alike find protection on British soil.

The panting bondmen have always found a sure refuge in Canada, and yearly our labor has been sought by Englishmen for the West Indies. The doors, therefore, are wide open in these civilized lands, thank God. Under the laws of Great Britain, colored men are neither debarred from citizenship nor soldier's rights and duties when their services are required.

That it is hard for those who have all their lives been submitting to the wrongs heaped upon the black man, or identified with parties oppressing him, now in this fearful crisis to make the marvelous change that justice demands, none can question.

A very appropriate paragraph occurs in a letter from a friend, which came to hand months back, which I will here quote:

"Has slavery so paralyzed the arm of the nation, that there is no strength to grapple with it? Is there not a story told of a man who fell asleep in an arbor, to whose entrance came a snake so surcharged with venom that the man died poisoned by its breath? Does not the state of our country suggest a parallel case, poisoned to its heart's deep core by its guilty contact with slavery?"

In these remarks, though coming from one of the race considered to be inferior, lies in a nutshell the grand secret of all the nation's trouble. And it seems reasonable to infer that the nation shall not again have peace and prosperity until prejudice, selfishness and slavery are sorely punished in the nation.

SOURCE: *Lift Every Voice: African American Oratory 1787–1900* by Philip S. Foner and Robert J. Branham. Copyright 1998 by the University of Alabama Press. Reprinted by permission.

EMILY DICKINSON

How deeply the Civil War penetrated even the most reclusive lives is apparent in this poem by Emily Dickinson. She seldom left her home but the war came to her through the daily newspaper, her brother's purchase of a substitute for $500 to fight for him, and the deaths of friends and sons of friends. Her preoccupation with death, especially in 1862, her most prolific year of composition, may indicate not morbidity, but rather a confrontation with reality during the Civil War.

ALONG THE POTOMAC

WHEN I was small, a woman
   died.
  To-day her only boy
Went up from the Potomac,
His face all victory,

To look at her; how slowly
The seasons must have turned
Till bullets clipt an angle,
And he passed quickly round!

If pride shall be in Paradise
I never can decide;
Of their imperial conduct,
No person testified.

But proud in apparition,
That woman and her boy
Pass back and forth before my
   brain,
As ever in the sky.

Emily Dickinson's unusual capitalization and punctuation were regularized in this collection of poems, edited by two of her friends. They also added the title.

SOURCE: *Poems*, edited by Mabel Loomis Todd and T. W. Higginson (Boston, 1892).

HERMAN MELVILLE

Naval operations were vital to the war and resulted in Union strongholds in coastal South Carolina and New Orleans and a federal blockade of the Mississippi River until only one third of southern maritime trade continued to function. One of the most famous naval encounters was that of two ironclad ships, the Confederate Virginia *(formerly the* Merrimack*) and the Union* Monitor. *After several hours of fighting, the* Virginia *wounded the* Monitor, *but later refused to resume fighting when rechallenged by the northern vessel. Although neither ship ever fought again, naval engagements would never be the same. Herman Melville's poem muses on the impact of their technological innovations on warfare.*

A UTILITARIAN VIEW OF THE *MONITOR*'S FIGHT

(1862)

Plain be the phrase, yet apt the verse,
  More ponderous than nimble;
For since grimed War here laid aside
His Orient pomp, 'twould ill befit
    Overmuch to ply
  The rhyme's barbaric cymbal.

Hail to victory without the gaud
  Of glory; zeal that needs no fans
Of banners; plain mechanic power
Plied cogently in War now placed-
    Where War belongs—
  Among the trades and artisans.

Yet this was battle, and intense—
  Beyond the strife of fleets heroic;
Deadlier, closer, calm 'mid storm;
No passion; all went on by crank,
    Pivot, and screw,
  And calculations of caloric.

Needless to dwell; the story's known.
  The ringing of those plates on plates
Still ringeth round the world—
The clangor of that blacksmith's fray.
    The anvil-din
  Resounds this message from the Fates:

War shall yet be, and to the end;
  But war-paint shows the streaks of weather;
War yet shall be; but warriors
Are now but operatives; War's made
    Less grand than Peace,
And a singe runs through lace and feather.

SOURCE: *Battle-Pieces and Aspects of the War*
(New York, 1866).

CHARLES MINOR BLACKFORD

The Confederate soldier Charles Blackford relates, in evocative detail, scenes of high glory and sorrowful routine. He captures the frustration with military bureaucracy and delineates the class distinctions dividing troops as well as common virtues that transcend rank and enemy.

LETTERS

[*Near Richmond*] *July 15, 1862* . . . I was invited by Colonel A.S. Pendleton, . . . to go with General Jackson and his staff into town this morning, and of course I was proud to be of so distinguished a party, though a very small atom in it. We went first to the Governor's mansion, where, by appointment I suppose, we met General Lee. . . . Lee was elegantly dressed in full uniform, sword and sash, spotless boots, beautiful spurs and was by far the most magnificent looking man I ever saw; the highest type of the cavalier class to which by blood and rearing he belongs. Jackson, a typical round head, on the other hand, was poorly dressed, that is he looked so, though of course his clothes were made of good material. His cap was very indifferent and pulled down over one eye, much stained by weather and without insignia of rank or corps which was visible. His coat was closely buttoned up to the chin and had upon the collar the stars and wreath of a general. His shoulders were stooped and one was lower than the other, and his coat showed the signs of much exposure to the weather. . . .

[*Slaughter Mountain*] *August 16,* . . . I was just at the point where troops who were going into the fight were thrown from column into line of battle. Here . . . I saw what I had never seen before—the men pinning strips of paper to their coats, with their name, company and regiment marked on them, so they could be identified if killed.

After standing at this point a long time, . . . the firing in my front and to the left of the road became very sharp and was nearing me rapidly, showing that our men had either been driven or were falling back . . . but in an instant a regiment or two burst through into the open spot where I was standing, all out of order and mixed up with a great number of yankees. I could not understand it; I could not tell whether our men had captured the yankees or the yankees had broken our line. In an instant, however, the doubt was put at rest, for General Jackson, with one or two of his staff, came dashing across the road from our right in great haste and excitement. As he got amongst the disordered troops he drew his sword and then reached over and took his battle-flag from my man, Bob Isbell, who was carrying it, and, dropping his bridle-rein, waved it over his head, and at the same time cried out in a loud voice: "Rally, men! Remember Winder! Where's my Stonewall Brigade!! Forward men! Forward!!" As he did so he dashed to the front, and our men followed with a yell and drove everything before them. It was a wonderful scene—one which men do not often see. Jackson, usually, is an indifferent and slouchy-looking man, but then, with "the light of battle" shedding its radiance over him, his whole person was changed. His action was as graceful as Lee's and his face was lit with the inspiration of heroism. The men would have followed him into the jaws of death itself; nothing could have stopped them, and nothing did. Even the old sorrel seemed endowed with the style and form of an Arabian.

Just as this wonderful scene was being enacted a very handsome and hatless yankee captain, not over twenty-one or two years of age, whose head was covered with clusters of really golden curls, and who had in his hand a broken sword, showing that he had led the gallant charge which had broken our ranks, laid his hand on my knee as I sat on my horse and said, with great emotion, "What officer is that, Captain?" and when I told him, fully appreciating the magnetism of the occasion, he seemed carried away with admiration, and, with that touch of nature which makes all the world a-kin, he waved his broken sword around his head and shouted, "Hurrah for Stonewall Jackson! Follow your General, boys!" I leaned over and, almost with tears in my eyes, said, "You are too good a fellow for me to make a prisoner; take that path to the left and you can escape." He saluted me with his broken sword, and disappeared in an instant. I hope he escaped.

SOURCE: *Memoirs of Life In and Out of the Army in*
Virginia During the War Between the States
(Lynchburg, Va., 1894–96).

L. MARIA CHILD

In 1833, white abolitionist Lydia Maria Child wrote the
first book-length argument against slavery, Appeal in
Favor of That Class of Americans Called Africans, *a rad-*

ical position at that early time. Although exiled from major northern publishing circles for years, Child continued writing and working for the abolitionist cause as well as for native Americans and women. In the work published in 1863 that is reprinted here, her choice of purely economic rationales responded to the national quandary over whether private property, virtually sanctified in American culture, could be violated for the sake of individual rights.

from THE RIGHT WAY THE SAFE WAY, PROVED BY EMANCIPATION IN THE BRITISH WEST INDIES, AND ELSEWHERE

CHAPTER VII.
CONCLUDING REMARKS.

. . . Free labor has so obviously the advantage, in all respects, over slave labor, that posterity will marvel to find in the history of the nineteenth century any record of a system so barbarous, so clumsy, and so wasteful. Let us make a very brief comparison. The slave is bought, sometimes at a very high price; in free labor there is no such investment of capital. The slave does not care how slowly or carelessly he works; it is the freeman's interest to do his work well and quickly. The slave is indifferent how many tools he spoils; the freeman has a motive to be careful. The slave's clothing is indeed very cheap, but it is provided to him by his master, and it is of no consequence to him how fast it is destroyed; the hired laborer pays more for his garments, but he has a motive for making them last six times as long. The slave contrives to spend as much time as he can in the hospital; the free laborer has no time to spare to be sick. Hopeless poverty and a sense of being unjustly dealt by, impels the slave to steal from his master, and he has no social standing to lose by indulging the impulse; with the freeman pride of character is a powerful inducement to be honest. A salary must be paid to an overseer to compel the slave to work; the freeman is impelled by a desire to increase his property, and add to the comforts of himself and family. We should question the sanity of a man who took the main-spring out of his watch, and hired a boy to turn the hands round. Yet he who takes from laborers the natural and healthy stimulus of wages, and attempts to supply its place by the driver's whip, pursues a course quite as irrational.

When immediate emancipation is proposed, those who think loosely are apt to say, "But would you turn the slaves loose upon society?" There is no sense in such a question. Emancipated slaves are restrained from crime by the same laws that restrain other men; and experience proves that a consciousness of being *protected* by legislation inspires them with *respect* for the laws.

But of all common questions, it seems to me the most absurd one is, "What would you *do* with the slaves, if they were emancipated?" There would be no occasion for doing *any* thing with them. Their labor is needed where they are; and if white people can get along with them, under all the disadvantages and dangers of slavery, what should hinder their getting along under a system that would make them work better and faster, while it took from them all motive to rebellion?

It is often asked, "What is your plan?" It is a very simple one; but it would prove as curative as the prophet's direction, "Go wash, and be clean." It is merely to stimulate laborers by wages, instead of driving them by the whip. When that plan is once adopted, education and religious teaching, and agricultural improvements will soon follow, as matters of course.

It is not to be supposed that the transition from slavery to freedom would be unattended with inconveniences. All changes in society involve some disadvantages, either to classes or individuals. Even the introduction of a valuable machine disturbs for a while the relations of labor and capital But it is important to bear in mind that *whatever difficulties might attend emancipation would be slight and temporary; while the difficulties and dangers involved in the continuance of slavery are permanent, and constantly increasing. . . .*

SOURCE: *The Right Way The Safe Way, Proved by Emancipation in the British West Indies, and Elsewhere* (New York, 1862).

SARAH PARKER REMOND

Great Britain depended economically on cotton from the American South for their huge textile industry and was, therefore, inclined to give diplomatic recognition to the Confederate States of America. Black abolitionists from the United States such as Sarah Parker Remond lectured the British public repeatedly, increasing their sympathy for emancipation. Britain never did acknowledge the Confederacy as a separate nation. She delivered this speech in London in late 1862.

THE NEGROES IN
THE UNITED STATES OF AMERICA

. . . It has always been exceedingly difficult to ascertain the exact number of slaves in the Southern states; the usual estimate is about four and a half millions. These human chattels are but property in the estimation of slave-holders, and receive by public opinion, established custom, and law, only the protection which is generally given to animals. From the son of a southern slaveholder, Mr. H. R. Helper of North Carolina, we have the number of slaves in the Southern states:—These human chattels, the property of three hundred and forty-seven thousand slaveowners, constitute the basis of the working class of the entire south; in fact, they are the bone and sinew of all that makes the south prosperous, the producers of a large proportion of the material wealth, and of some of the most important articles of consumption produced by any working class in the world. The New Orleans *Delta* gives the following:—"The cotton plantations in the south are about eighty thousand, and the aggregate value of their annual product, at the present prices of cotton (before the civil war) is fully one hundred and twenty-five millions of dollars. There are over fifteen thousand tobacco plantations, and their annual products may be valued at fourteen millions of dollars. There are two thousand six hundred sugar plantations, the products of which average annually more than twelve millions of dollars." Add to this the domestic labour of the slaves as household servants &c., and you have some conception of the material wealth produced by the men and women termed chattels. The bulk of this money goes to the support of the slaveholders and their families; therefore the dependence of slaveholders upon their chattels is complete. Slave labour was first applied to the cultivation of tobacco, and afterwards to that of rice; but rice is produced only in a very limited locality; cotton is the great staple and source of prosperity and wealth, the nucleus around which gathers immense interests. Thousands among the commercial, manufacturing, and working classes, on both sides of the Atlantic, are dependent upon cotton for all material prosperity; but the slaves who have produced two-thirds of the cotton do not own themselves; their nominal wives and their children may at any moment be sold. I call them nominal *wives*, because there is no such thing as legal marriage permitted either by custom or law. The free operatives of Britain are, in reality, brought into almost personal relations with slaves during their daily toil. They manufacture the material which the slaves have produced, and although three thousand miles of ocean roll between the producer and the manufacturer and the operatives, they should call to mind the fact, that the cause of all the present internal struggle, now going on between the northern states and the south, the civil war and its attendant evils, have resulted from the attempt to perpetuate negro slavery. In a country like England, where the manufacturer pays in wages alone 11,000,000 [pounds], and the return from the cotton trade is about 80,000,000 [pounds] annually—where four millions of the population are almost directly interested—where starvation threatens thousands—it is well that the only remedy which can produce desirable and lasting prosperity should receive the moral support of every class—*emancipation*.

Let no diplomacy of statesmen, no intimidation of slaveholders, no scarcity of cotton, no fear of slave insurrections, prevent the people of Great Britain from maintaining their position as the friend of the oppressed negro, which they deservedly occupied previous to the disastrous civil war. The negro, and the nominally free coloured men and women, north and south, of the States, in every hour of their adversity, have ever relied upon the hope that the moral support of Britain would always be with the oppressed. . . .

EMILY AND DAVID GOLIGHTLY HARRIS

Emily Harris and her husband David owned a little over five hundred acres of farmland in the Piedmont region of South Carolina, which they cultivated with the help of ten enslaved workers. Their farming responsibilities and seven children kept David from joining the Confederate army until the threat of conscription forced him to "volunteer" for six months, after which he went back to the farm. He returned briefly to military service and then bought a substitute so he could rejoin his family. This episodic experience of military service was not unusual. But even David's frequent stays at home did not preserve the family from hardship. In these journals husband and wife record their anxieties and concerns.

DECEMBER ENTRIES

Emily Harris

December 5. Night has at last put an end to a very troublesome day. I have had company last night and to day. It has rained all day, the children have been cross and ungovernable. Old Judah and Edom are both sick. Ann is trying to weave, and a poor weave it is, the sewing must be done, every thing must be attended to; Laura is coughing a rough ominous cough, has scarcely any shoes on her feet, and no hope of getting any this week, West has the croup. I am trying to wean the baby and the cows laid out last night, and last and worst of all I know my husband is somewhere miserably cold, wet, and comfortless.

David Golightly Harris

December 6. Applying for, and receiving a furlough, I posted home to day. With the exception of a run off this morning we all came safely home. Our Regment are in a state of confusion, and we are waiting to see what the legislature will do with us. . . .

December 14. Sunday. A beautiful morning. Everything so fair, so beautiful & so pleasant. Yesterday, I passed the day at the village. Today, I am prepairing to start for the army, which is now in Charlestown. The redgement was in Columbia when I got my furlough. I have been violating the sabath by making a provision base to take with me. Wife & I am going to the village to day, so that I can take the cars in the morning. To day I will bid my children farewell again.

Emily Harris

December 14. At home. Husband gone to the army again, every thing resting on me, children troublesome, company forever, weather very cold, negroes in the newground, cows, calves and sheep on the wheat. To day I have heard that the Yankees were sheelling Charleston. Oh! God preserve my husband!

December 17. Weather excessively cold. Anxiously expecting news from Charleston. Mother almost insane. Negroes in the new ground and killing a beef. I almost wretched. . . .

December 24. Christmas eve! How different from any that I have spent. War raging in the land. Husband away in the camp. [I am] afraid to look into the "dark and shadowy future." Had a stack of hay hauled from forest bottom. Sent York with the four eldest children in the rockaway to the village to spend the night and Christmas day. Let them have pleasure while they can. A kind and merciful God is over us all.

SOURCE: *Piedmont Farmer: The Journals of David Golightly Harris*, edited by Philip N. Racine (Knoxville, Tenn., 1990).

SECTION 3 1863

For the North what began as a war to preserve the Union by 1863 had turned into a war to abolish slavery as well. The South began the war for liberty but their goal of achieving a separate nation was beginning to look less attainable. After the Union victories at Gettysburg and Vicksburg on July 3, 1863, the Confederate forces were weakened on the battlefield. The Battle of Gettysburg forced Lee to retreat from Union territory. Capturing Vicksburg was an enormous strategic victory for the North because it divided the South, gave the Union control of the Mississippi River, and reconnected the Midwest with the northern states. The southern troops, however, were not ready to quit, and they planned to continue fighting until northern interest in the war dissipated or at least until the election of 1864 when perhaps a Peace Democrat open to compromise with the Confederacy might be elected President.

In general, 1863 was a year of celebration and mourning. As these readings demonstrate, many abolitionists heralded President Lincoln for issuing the Emancipation Proclamation and for recognizing the right to freedom of the black population. Yet not all northerners rejoiced, and, after the Battle of Gettysburg, draft riots and lynchings occurred in several cities to protest free blacks entering the workforce. The whole country mourned the loss of thousands of lives, but the war was far from over. Civilians continued to fear or experience dislocation from their homes and the loss of family and friends. Hunger, rationing, poverty, illness, and inflation took their toll on civilians and soldiers alike.

ABRAHAM LINCOLN

Drafted in July 1862 and preliminarily issued in September of that year, the Emancipation Proclamation finally took effect on January 1, 1863. Since the southern states did not rejoin the Union by the deadline imposed by this proclamation, the mission of federal forces attempting to restore the Union would now also include recognizing the freedom of all the people held in slavery. But the Emancipation Proclamation did not apply to any slave-master in the border states and certain other territories which remained in the Union, nor did it immediately free any slaves. The document did, however, have the psychological effect of validating the abolitionist cause and the enslaved people's hope.

EMANCIPATION PROCLAMATION

Whereas, on the 22nd day of September, in the year of our Lord one thousand eight hundred and sixty-two, a proclamation was issued by the President of the United States, containing, among other things, the following, to wit:—

That on the first day of January, in the year of our Lord one thousand eight hundred and sixty-three, all persons held as slaves within any States or designated part of a State, the people whereof shall then be in rebellion against the United States, shall be then, thenceforward, and forever free; and the Executive Government of the United States, including the military and naval authority thereof, will recognize and maintain the freedom of such persons, and will do no act or acts to repress such persons, or any of them, in any efforts they may make for their actual freedom.

That the Executive will, on the first day of January aforesaid, by proclamation, designate the States and parts of States, if any, in which the people thereof respectively shall then be in rebellion against the United States; and the fact that any State, or the people thereof, shall on that day be in good faith represented in the Congress of the United

States, by members chosen thereto at elections wherein a majority of the qualified voters of such State shall have participated, shall, in the absence of strong countervailing testimony, be deemed conclusive evidence that such State, and the people thereof, are not then in rebellion against the United States.

Now, therefore, I, Abraham Lincoln, President of the United States, by virtue of the power in me vested as commander-in-chief of the army and navy of the United States in time of actual armed rebellion against the authority and Government of the United States, and as a fit and necessary war measure for suppressing said rebellion, do, on this first day of January, in the year of our Lord one thousand eight hundred and sixty-three, and in accordance with my purpose so to do, publicly proclaimed for the full period of one hundred days from the day first above mentioned, order and designate, as the States and parts of States wherein the people thereof respectively are this day in rebellion against the United States, the following, to wit:

Arkansas, Texas, Louisiana (except the parishes of St. Bernard, Plaquemines, Jefferson, St. John, St. Charles, St. James, Ascension, Assumption, Terre Bonne, Lafourche, Ste. Marie, St. Martin, and Orleans, including the City of New Orleans), Mississippi, Alabama, Florida, Georgia, South Carolina, North Carolina, and Virginia (except the forty-eight counties designated as West Virginia, and also the counties of Berkeley, Accomac, Northampton, Elizabeth City, York, Princess Anne, and Norfolk, including the cities of Norfolk and Portsmouth), and which excepted parts are for the present left precisely as if this proclamation were not issued.

And by virtue of the power and for the purpose aforesaid, I do order and declare that all persons held as slaves within said designated States and parts of States are, and henceforward shall be, free; and that the Executive Government of the United States, including the military and naval authorities thereof, will recognize and maintain the freedom of said persons.

And I hereby enjoin upon the people so declared to be free to abstain from all violence, unless in necessary self-defence; and I recommend to them that, in all cases when allowed, they labor faithfully for reasonable wages.

And I further declare and make known that such persons, of suitable condition, will be received into the armed service of the United States, to garrison forts, positions, stations, and other places, and to man vessels of all sorts in said service.

And upon this act, sincerely believed to be an act of justice, warranted by the Constitution upon military necessity, I invoke the considerate judgment of mankind, and the gracious favor of Almighty God.

In testimony whereof, I have hereunto set my name, and caused the seal of the United States to be affixed.

Done at the city of Washington, this first day of January, in the year of our Lord one thousand eight hundred and sixty-three, and of the independence of the United States the eighty-seventh.

By the President: ABRAHAM LINCOLN.
  WILLIAM H. SEWARD, Secretary of State.

SOURCE: *The Life and Public Services of Abraham Lincoln* by Henry J. Raymond (New York, 1865).

CHARLOTTE FORTEN

When the Emancipation Proclamation officially took effect, numerous jubilee celebrations erupted among blacks in territories under Union control. Charlotte Forten, a northern black teacher in South Carolina, recounted in her diary her participation in the New Year's Day festivities on the Sea Islands in Port Royal Sound.

NEW YEAR'S DAY—EMANCIPATION DAY

New-Year's-Day—Emancipation-Day—was a glorious one to us. The morning was quite cold, the coldest we had experienced; but we were determined to go to the celebration at Camp Saxton, . . . whither the General and Colonel Higginson had bidden us, on this, "the greatest day in the nation's history." We enjoyed perfectly the exciting scene on board the Flora. There was an eager, wondering crowd of the freed people in their holiday-attire, with the gayest of head-handkerchiefs, the whitest of aprons, and the happiest of faces. The band was playing, the flags streaming, everybody talking merrily and feeling strangely happy. The sun shone brightly, the very waves seemed to partake of the universal gayety, and danced and sparkled more joyously than ever before. Long before we reached Camp Saxton we could see the beautiful grove, and the ruins of the old Huguenot fort near it. Some companies of the First Regiment were drawn up in line under the trees, near the landing, to receive us. A fine, soldierly-looking set of men; their brilliant dress against the trees (they were then wearing red pantaloons) invested them with a semi-barbaric splendor. It was my good fortune to find among the officers an old friend,—and what it was to meet a friend from the North, in our isolated Southern life, no one can imagine who has not experienced the pleasure. Letters were an unspeakable luxury,—we hungered for them, we could never get enough; but to meet old friends,—that was "too much, too much" as the people here say, when they are very much in earnest. . . .

The celebration took place in the beautiful grove of live-oaks adjoining the camp. . . . I wish it were possible to describe fitly the scene which met our eyes as we sat upon the stand, and looked down on the crowd before us. There were the black soldiers in their blue coats and scarlet pantaloons, the officers of this and other regiments in their handsome uniforms, and crowds of lookers-on,—men, women, and children, of every complexion, grouped in various attitudes under the moss-hung trees. The faces of all wore a happy, interested look. The exercises commenced with a prayer by the chaplain of the regiment. . . . Colonel Higginson then introduced Dr. Brisbane, who read the President's Proclamation, which was enthusiastically cheered. Rev. Mr. French presented to the Colonel two very elegant flags, a gift to the regiment from the Church of the Puritans, accompanying them by an appropriate and enthusiastic speech. At its conclusion, before Colonel Higginson could reply, and while he still stood holding the flags in his hand, some of the colored people, of their own accord, commenced singing, "My Country, 't is of thee." It was a touching and beautiful incident, and sent a thrill through all our hearts. The Colonel was deeply moved by it. He said that that reply was far more effective than any speech he could make. . . .

After the meeting we saw the dress-parade, a brilliant and beautiful sight. An officer told us that the men went through the drill remarkably well,—that the ease and rapidity with which they learned the movements were wonderful. To us it seemed strange as a miracle,—this black regiment, the first mustered into the service of the United States, doing itself honor in the sight of the officers of other regiments, many of whom, doubtless, "came to scoff." The men afterwards had a great feast, ten oxen having been roasted whole for their especial benefit. . . .

It was the softest, loveliest moonlight; we seated ourselves on the ruined wall of the old fort; and when the boat had got a short distance from the shore the band in it commenced playing "Sweet Home." The moonlight on the water, the perfect stillness around, the wildness and solitude of the ruins, all seemed to give new pathos to that ever dear and beautiful old song. It came very near to all of us,—strangers in that strange Southern land. . . . Very unwilling were we to go home; for, besides the attractive society, we knew that the soldiers were to have grand shouts and a general jubilee that night. But the Flora was coming, and we were obliged to say a reluctant farewell to Camp Saxton and the hospitable dwellers therein, and hasten to the landing. We promenaded the deck of the steamer, sang patriotic songs, and agreed that moonlight and water had never looked so beautiful as on that night. At Beaufort we took the row-boat for St. Helena; and the boat-men, as they rowed, sang some of their sweetest, wildest hymns. It was a fitting close to such a day. Our hearts were filled with an exceeding great gladness; for, although the Government had left much undone, we knew that Freedom was surely born in our land that day. . . .

SOURCE: *Atlantic Monthly*
(June 1864).

J. B. JONES

Not only soldiers, but also farmers and wives and moth-ers suffered from the economic hardships of wartime. Rising costs of living, cheap paper money issued freely by the Confederate government, and Union blockade of rivers in a South lacking efficient transportation systems led to rationing and poverty even in the Confederate cap-ital of Richmond, Virginia. John Beauchamp Jones, a clerk in the War Department there, compares in his diary some everyday living expenses in 1863 with costs before the war. He blames the government for its inequitable distribution of supplies.

from A REBEL WAR CLERK'S DIARY

January 18th.—. . . We are now, in effect, in a state of siege, and none but the opulent, often those who have defrauded the govern-ment, can obtain a sufficiency of food and raiment. Calico, which could once be bought for 12 1/2 cts. per yard, is now selling at $2.25, and a lady's dress of calico costs her about $30.00. Bonnets are not to be had. Common bleached cotton shirting brings $1.50 per yard. All other dry goods are held in the same proportion. Common tallow can-dles are $1.25 per pound; soap, $1.00; hams, $1.00; opossum $3.00; turkeys $4 to $11.00; sugar, brown, $1.00; molasses $8.00 per gallon; potatoes $6.00 per bushel, etc.

These evils might be remedied by the government, for there is no great scarcity of any of the substantials and necessities of life in the country, if they were only equally distributed. The difficulty is in procuring transportation, and the government monopolizes the rail-roads and canals. . . .

February 11th.—. . . Some idea may be formed of the scarcity of food in this city from the fact that, while my youngest daughter was in the kitchen to-day, a young rat came out of its hole and seemed to beg for something to eat; she held out some bread, which it ate from her hand, and seemed grateful. Several others soon appeared, and were as tame as kittens. Perhaps we shall have to eat them! . . .

February 18th.—. . . One or two of the regiments of Gen. Lee's army were in the city last night. The men were pale and haggard. They have but a quarter of a pound of meat per day. But meat has been ordered from Atlanta. I hope it is abundant there.

All the necessaries of life in the city are still going up higher in price. Butter, $3 per pound; beef, $1; bacon, $1.25; sausage-meat, $1; and even liver is selling at 50 cents per pound.

By degrees, quite perceptible, we are approaching the condition of famine. What effect this will produce on the community is to be seen. The army must be fed or disbanded, or else the city must be abandoned. How we, "the people," are to live is a thought of serious concern. . . .

March 30th.—. . . The gaunt form of wretched famine still approaches with rapid strides. Meal is now selling at $12 per bushel, and potatoes at $16. Meats have almost disappeared from the market, and none but the opulent can afford to pay $3.50 per pound for butter. *Greens*, however, of various kinds, are coming in; and as the season advances, we may expect a diminution of prices. It is strange that on the 30th of March, even in the "sunny South," the fruit-trees are as bare of blossoms and foliage as at mid-winter. We shall have fire until the middle of May,—six months of winter!

I am spading up my little garden, and hope to raise a few vegetables to eke out a miserable subsistence for my family. My daughter Ann reads Shakespeare to me o' nights, which saves my eyes. . . .

April 17th.—. . . Pins are so scarce and costly, that it is now a pretty general practice to stoop down and pick up any found in the street. The boarding-houses are breaking up, and rooms, furnished and unfurnished, are renting out to messes. One dollar and fifty cents for beef, leaves no margin for profit, even at $100 per month, which is charged for board, and most of the boarders cannot afford to pay that price. Therefore they take rooms, and buy their own scanty food. I am inclined to think provisions would not be deficient, to an alarming extent, if they were equally distributed. Wood is no scarcer than before the war, and yet $30 per load (less than a cord) is demanded for it, and obtained. . . .

August 22nd.—Night before last all the clerks in the city post-office resigned, because the government did not give them salaries sufficient to subsist them. As yet their places have not been filled, and the government gets no letters—some of which lying in the office may be of such importance as to involve the safety or ruin of the government. Tomorrow is Sunday, and of course the mails will not be attended to before Monday—the letters lying here four days unopened! This really looks as if we had no Postmaster-General. . . .

October 22nd.—. . . A poor woman yesterday applied to a merchant in Carey Street to purchase a barrel of flour. The price he demanded was $70.

"My God!" exclaimed she, "how can I pay such prices? I have seven children; what shall I do?"

"I don't know, madam," said he, coolly, "unless you eat your children."

Such is the power of cupidity—it transforms men into demons. And if this spirit prevails throughout the country, a just God will bring calamities upon the land, which will reach these cormorants, but which, it may be feared, will involve all classes in a common ruin. . . .

SOURCE: *A Rebel War Clerk's Diary*
(Philadelphia, 1866).

EMILY DICKINSON

Noted for her originality of insight and phrasing, the Massachusetts poet Emily Dickinson grapples with another facet of the national experience, the sudden departure of a cherished friend and her fear that he will die. Her letter is addressed to T. W. Higginson, a white officer who led the 1st South Carolina Volunteers, a regiment of black soldiers mustered into the Union army in January 1863.

LETTER TO MR. T. W. HIGGINSON

[February 1863]
Amherst

DEAR FRIEND, — I did not deem that planetary forces annulled, but suffered an exchange of territory, or world.

I should have liked to see you before you became improbable. War feels to me an oblique place. Should there be other summers, would you perhaps come?

I found you were gone, by accident, as I find systems are, or sea-

sons of the year, and obtain no cause, but suppose it a treason of progress that dissolves as it goes. Carlo* still remained, and I told him
>Best gains must have the losses' test,
>To constitute them gains.

My shaggy ally assented.

Perhaps death gave me awe for friends, striking sharp and early, for I held them since in a brittle love, of more alarm than peace. I trust you may pass the limit of war; and though not reared to prayer, when service is had in church for our arms, I include yourself. . . . I was thinking to-day, as I noticed, that the 'supernatural' was only the natural disclosed.
>Not 'Revelation' 't is that waits,
>But our unfurnished eyes.

But I fear I detain you. Should you, before this reaches you, experience Immortality, who will inform me of the exchange? Could you, with honor, avoid death, I entreat you, sir. It would bereave.
>YOUR GNOME.

SOURCE: *Letters of Emily Dickinson,*
edited by Mabel Loomis Todd
(Boston, 1894).

ROBERT PURVIS

By spring 1863, more blacks were being recruited into the Union army and rejoicing at the new rights some could exercise since the Emancipation Proclamation. Robert Purvis, an abolitionist, was the son of a wealthy white Charleston merchant and a free black woman. He gave this speech at the thirtieth annual meeting of the American Anti-Slavery Society in New York City on May 12, 1863, celebrating the change in the course of the treatment of blacks in the territories under Union control.

SPEECH, MAY 12, 1863

. . . Mr. Chairman, this is a proud day for the "colored" man. For the first time since this Society was organized, I stand before you a recognized citizen of the United States. And, let me add, for the first time since your government was a government, it is an honor to be a

---

*Emily's dog

citizen of the United States! Sir, old things are passing away, all things are becoming new. Now a black man has rights, under this government, which every white man, here and everywhere, is bound to respect. The damnable doctrine of the detestable Taney is no longer the doctrine of the country. The Slave Power no longer rules at Washington. The slaveholders and their miserable allies are biting the dust. . . . The black man is a citizen—all honor to Secretary Bates, who has so pronounced him! The black man can take out a passport, and travel to the uttermost parts of the earth, protected by the broad aegis of the government—all honor to Secretary Seward, who was the first to recognize this right! The black man is a citizen soldier, standing on an equality in the rank and file with the white soldier—all honor to Secretary Stanton and the rest of the Administration! Sir, I know very well that this government is not yet all that it ought to be. . . . But, sir, these gentlemen have in a signal manner recognized my rights, and the rights of my oppressed countrymen. They have officially invested us with the prerogatives of which we have been basely robbed, and I would be false to my nature, false to my convictions, false to my best feelings, did I not thus publicly testify my sense of respect and heartfelt gratitude. . . . I have said that I consider it an honor to be a citizen of this republic, and I repeat it. I am proud to be an American citizen. You know, Mr. Chairman, how bitterly I used to denounce the United States as the basest despotism the sun ever shone upon; and I take nothing back that ever I said. When this government was, as it used to be, a slave-holding oligarchy . . . I hated it with a wrath which words could not express, and I denounced it with all the bitterness of my indignant soul. . . . I was a victim, stricken, degraded, injured, insulted in my person, in my family, in my friends, in my estate; I returned bitterness for bitterness, and scorn for scorn. . . . I forget the past; joy fills my soul at the prospect of the future. . . . But, I hear some of my hearers saying, "It is too soon to begin to rejoice; don't halloo till you are out of the woods; don't be too sure of the future—wait and see." No, sir, I will not wait—I cannot be mistaken. My instincts, in this matter at least, are unerring. The good time which has so long been coming is at hand. I feel it, I see it in the air, I read it in the signs of the times; I see it in the acts of Congress, in the abolition of slavery in the District of Columbia, in its exclusion from the Territories, in solemn treaties for the effectual suppression of the infernal foreign slave trade, in the acknowledgment of the black republics of Hayti and Liberia. I see it in the new spirit that is in the army; I see it in the black regiment of South Carolina—I see it in the 54th Regiment of Massachusetts; I see it in the order of Adjutant-General Thomas, forming a black brigade at Memphis; I see it, above all, and more than all, in *the glorious and immortal proclamation of Abraham Lincoln on the first of*

January, 1863. By that imperishable instrument, the three million of slaves in the rebel States are legally and irrevocably free! . . . By that immortal document, all the remaining slaves of the country are in effect promised their freedom. In *spirit* and in *purpose*, thanks to *Almighty God!* this is no longer a slaveholding republic. The fiat has gone forth which, when this rebellion is crushed . . . in the simple but beautiful language of the President, "will take all burdens from off all backs, and make every man a freeman."

. . . Our country is not yet free, but thank God for those signs of the times that unmistakably indicate that it soon will be! . . .

SOURCE: *The Liberator*
(May 22, 1863).

MARY ANN LOUGHBOROUGH

The inhabitants of Vicksburg, a city under siege for forty-eight days by federal forces commanded by Ulysses S. Grant and defended by troops led by John C. Pemberton, were forced to vacate their homes. Caves were built into the hillsides surrounding this Mississippi town and people set up residence in them until the Confederate army surrendered to Union troops on July 4, 1863. Mary Ann Loughborough describes what it was like to try to make a home for herself and her family in one of these caves.

from MY CAVE LIFE IN VICKSBURG

. . . The discharges of musketry were irregular. . . . At every report our hearts beat quicker. The excitement was intense in the city. Groups of people stood on every available position where a view could be obtained of the distant hills, where the jets of white smoke constantly passed out from among the trees.

Some of our friends proposed going for a better view up on the balcony around the cupola of the court house. The view from there was most extensive and beautiful. Hill after hill arose in the distance, enclosing the city in the form of a crescent. Immediately in the centre and east of the river, the firing seemed more continuous, while to the left and running northly, the rattle and roar would be sudden, sharp, and vigorous, then ceasing for some time. The hills around near the city, and indeed every place that seemed commanding and secure, was covered with anxious spectators—many of them ladies—fearing the result of the afternoon's conflict. . . .

It was amid the clump of trees on the far distant hillside, that the Federal batteries could be discerned by the frequent puffings of smoke from the guns. Turning to the river, we could see a gunboat that had the temerity to come down as near the town as possible, and lay just out of reach of the Confederate batteries, with steam up.

Two more lay about half a mile above and nearer the canal; two or three transports had gotten up steam, and lay near the mouth of the canal. Below the city a gunboat had come up and landed, out of reach, on the Louisiana side, striving to engage the lower batteries of the town—firing about every fifteen minutes. . . .

From gentlemen who called on the evening of the attack in the rear of the town, we learned that it was quite likely, judging from the movements on the river, that the gunboats would make an attack that night. We remained dressed during the night; once or twice we sprang to our feet, startled by the report of a cannon; but after waiting in the darkness of the veranda for some time, the perfect quiet of the city convinced us that our alarm was needless.

Next day, two or three shells were thrown from the battle field, exploding near the house. This was our first shock, and a severe one. We did not dare to go in the back part of the house all day. . . .

In the evening we were terrified and much excited by the loud rush and scream of mortar shells; we ran to the small cave near the house, and were in it during the night, by this time wearied and almost stupefied by the loss of sleep.

The caves were plainly becoming a necessity, as some persons had been killed on the street by fragments of shells. The room that I had so lately slept in had been struck by a fragment of a shell during the first night, and a large hole made in the ceiling. I shall never forget my extreme fear during the night, and my utter hopelessness of ever seeing the morning light. Terror stricken, we remained crouched in the cave, while shell after shell followed each other in quick succession. I endeavored by constant prayer to prepare myself for the sudden death I was almost certain awaited me. My heart stood still as we would hear the reports from the guns, and the rushing and fearful sound of the shell as it came toward us. As it neared, the noise became more deafening; the air was full of the rushing sound; pains darted through my temples; my ears were full of the confusing noise; and, as it exploded, the report flashed through my head like an electric shock, leaving me in a quiet state of terror the most painful that I can imagine—cowering in a corner, holding my child to my heart—the only feeling of my life being the choking throbs of my heart, that rendered me almost breathless. As singly they fell short, or beyond the cave, I was aroused by a feeling of thankfulness that was of short duration. Again and again the terrible fright came over us in that night.

I saw one fall in the road without the mouth of the cave, like a flame of fire, making the earth tremble, and, with a low, singing sound, the fragments sped on in their work of death.

Morning found us more dead than alive, with blanched faces and trembling lips. We were not reassured on hearing, from a man who took refuge in the cave, that a mortar shell in falling would not consider the thickness of earth above us a circumstance.

Some of the ladies, more courageous by daylight, asked him what he was in there for, if that was the case. He was silenced for an hour, when he left. As the day wore on, and we were still preserved, though the shells came as ever, we were somewhat encouraged.

The next morning we heard that Vicksburg would not in all probability hold out more than a week or two, as the garrison was poorly provisioned; and one of General Pemberton's staff officers told us that the effective force of the garrison, upon being estimated, was found to be fifteen thousand men; General Loring having been cut off after the battle of Black River, with probably ten thousand.

The ladies all cried, "Oh, never surrender!" but after the experience of the night, I really could not tell what I wanted, or what my opinions were. . . .

So constantly dropped the shells around the city, that the inhabitants all made preparations to live under the ground during the siege. M— sent over and had a cave made in a hill near by. We seized the opportunity one evening, when the gunners were probably at their supper, for we had a few moments of quiet, to go over and take possession. We were under the care of a friend of M—, who was paymaster on the staff of the same General with whom M— was Adjutant. We had neighbors on both sides of us; and it would have been an amusing sight to a spectator to witness the domestic scenes presented without by the number of servants preparing the meals under the high bank containing the caves.

Our dining, breakfasting, and supper hours were quite irregular. When the shells were falling fast, the servants came in for safety, and our meals waited for completion some little time; again they would fall slowly, with the lapse of many minutes between, and out would start the cooks to their work.

Some families had light bread made in large quantities, and subsisted on it with milk (provided their cows were not killed from one milking time to another), without any more cooking, until called on to replenish. Though most of us lived on corn bread and bacon, served three times a day, the only luxury of the meal consisting in its warmth, I had some flour, and frequently had some hard, tough biscuit made from it, there being no soda or yeast to be procured. At this time we could, also, procure beef. A gentleman friend was kind enough to offer me his camp bed, a narrow spring mattress, which fitted within the contracted cave very comfortably; another had his tent fly stretched over the mouth of our residence to shield us from the sun; and thus I was the recipient of many favors, and under obligations to many gentlemen of the army for delicate and kind attentions. . . . And so I went regularly to work, keeping house under ground. Our new habitation was an excavation made in the earth, and branching six feet from the entrance, forming a cave in the shape of a T. In one of the wings my bed fitted; the other I used as a kind of a dressing room; in this the earth had been cut down a foot or two below the floor of the main cave; I could stand erect here; and when tired of sitting in other portions of my residence, I bowed myself into it and stood impassively resting at full height—one of the variations in the still shell-expectant life. M—'s servant cooked for us under protection of the hill. Our quarters were close, indeed; yet I was more comfortable than I expected I could have been made under the earth in that fashion.

We were safe at least from fragments of shell—and they were flying in all directions; though no one seemed to think our cave any protection, should a mortar shell happen to fall directly on top of the ground above us. We had our roof arched and braced, the supports of the bracing taking up much room in our confined quarters. The earth was about five feet thick above, and seemed hard and compact; yet, poor M—, every time he came in, examined it, fearing, amid some of the shocks it sustained, that it might crack and fall upon us.

One afternoon, amid the rush and explosion of the shells, cries and screams arose—the screams of women amid the shrieks of the falling shells. The servant boy, George, after starting and coming back once or twice, his timidity overcoming his curiosity, . . . at last gathered courage to go to the ravine near us, from whence the cries proceeded, and found that a negro man had been buried alive within a cave, he being alone at that time. Workmen were instantly set to deliver him, if possible; but when found, the unfortunate man had evidently been dead some little time. . . .

Another incident happened the same day: A gentleman, resident of Vicksburg, had a large cave made, and repeatedly urged his wife to leave the house and go into it. She steadily refused, and, being quite an invalid, was lying on the bed, when he took her by the hand and insisted upon her accompanying him so strongly, that she yielded; and they had scarcely left the house, when a mortar shell went crashing through, utterly demolishing the bed that had so lately been vacated, tearing up the floor, and almost completely destroying the room.

That night, after my little one had been laid in bed, I sat at the mouth of the cave, with the servants drawn around me, watching the brilliant display of fireworks the mortar boats were making—the passage of the shell, as it travelled through the heavens, looking like a swiftly moving star. As it fell, it approached the earth so rapidly, that it seemed to leave behind a track of fire.

This night we kept our seats, as they all passed rapidly over us, none falling near. The incendiary shells were still more beautiful in appearance. As they exploded in the air, the burning matter and balls fell like large, clear blue-and-amber stars, scattering hither and thither.

"Miss M—," said one of the more timid servants, "do they want to kill us all dead? Will they keep doing this until we all die?"

I said most heartily, "I hope not."

The servants we had with us seemed to possess more courage than is usually attributed to negroes. They seldom hesitated to cross the street for water at any time. The "boy" slept at the entrance of the cave, with a pistol I had given him, telling me I need not be "afeared—dat any one dat come dar would have to go over his body first."

He never refused to carry out any little article to M— on the battle field. I laughed heartily at a dilemma he was placed in one day: The mule that he had mounted to ride out to the battle field took him to a dangerous locality, where the shells were flying thickly, and then, suddenly stopping, through fright, obstinately refused to stir. It was in vain that George kicked and beat him—go he would not; so, clenching his hand, he hit him severely in the head several times, jumped down, ran home, and left him. The mule stood a few minutes rigidly, then, looking round, and seeing George at some distance from him, turned and followed, quite demurely. . . .

Days wore on, and the mortar shells had passed over continually without falling near us; so that I became quite at my ease, in view of our danger, when one of the Federal batteries opposite the intrenchments altered their range; so that, at about six o'clock every evening, Parrott shells came whirring into the city, frightening the inhabitants of caves wofully. . . .

The cave we inhabited was about five squares from the levee. A great many had been made in a hill immediately beyond us; and near this hill we could see most of the shells fall. Caves were the fashion— the rage—over besieged Vicksburg. Negroes, who understood their business, hired themselves out to dig them, at from thirty to fifty dollars, according to the size. Many persons, considering different localities unsafe, would sell them to others, who had been less fortunate, or less provident; and so great was the demand for cave workmen, that a new branch of industry sprang up and became popular— particularly as the personal safety of the workmen was secured, and money withal. . . .

Even the very animals seemed to share the general fear of a sudden and frightful death. The dogs would be seen in the midst of the noise to gallop up the street, and then to return, as if fear had maddened them. On hearing the descent of a shell, they would dart aside—then, as it exploded, sit down and howl in the most pitiful manner. There were many walking the street, apparently without homes. George carried on a continual warfare with them, as they came about the fire where our meals were cooking. . . .

The horses, belonging to the officers, and fastened to the trees near the tents, would frequently strain the halter to its full length, rearing high in the air, with a loud snort of terror, as a shell would explode near. I could hear them in the night cry out in the midst of the uproar, ending in a low, plaintive whinny of fear.

The poor creatures subsisted entirely on cane tops and mulberry leaves. Many of the mules and horses had been driven outside of the lines, by order of General Pemberton, for subsistence. Only mules enough were left, belonging to the Confederacy, to allow three full teams to a regiment. Private property was not interfered with. . . .

The hill opposite our cave might be called "death's point" from the number of animals that had been killed in eating the grass on the sides and summit. In all directions I can see the turf turned up, from the shells that have gone ploughing into the earth. Horses or mules that are tempted to mount the hill by the promise of grass that grows profusely there, invariably come limping down wounded, to die at the base, or are brought down dead from the summit.

A certain number of mules are killed each day by the commissaries, and are issued to the men, all of whom prefer the fresh meat, though it be of mule, to the bacon and salt rations that they have eaten for so long a time without change. There have already been some cases of scurvy: the soldiers have a horror of the disease; therefore, I suppose, the mule meat is all the more welcome. Indeed, I petitioned M— to have some served on our table. He said: "No; wait a little longer." He did not like to see me eating mule until I was obliged to; that he trusted Providence would send us some change shortly.

. . . [N]ews came that one of the forts to the left of us had been undermined and blown up, killing sixty men; then of the death of the gallant Colonel Irwin, of Missouri; and again, the next day, of the death of the brave old General Green, of Missouri.

We were now swiftly nearing the end of our siege life: the rations had nearly all been given out. For the last few days I had been sick; still I tried to overcome the languid feeling of utter prostration. My little one had swung in her hammock, reduced in strength, with a low fever flushing in her face. M— was all anxiety, I could plainly see. A soldier brought up, one morning, a little jaybird, as a plaything for the child. After playing with it for a short time, she turned wearily away. "Miss Mary," said the servant, "she's hungry; let me make her some soup from the bird." At first I refused: the poor little plaything should not die; then, as I thought of the child, I half consented. With the utmost haste, Cinth disappeared; and the next time she appeared, it was with a cup of soup, and a little plate, on which lay the white meat of the poor little bird.

On Saturday a painful calm prevailed: there had been a truce proclaimed; and so long had the constant firing been kept up, that the stillness now was absolutely oppressive.

At ten o'clock General Bowen passed by, dressed in full uniform, accompanied by Colonel Montgomery, and preceded by a courier bearing a white flag. M— came by, and asked me if I would like to walk out; so I put on my bonnet and sullied forth beyond the terrace, for the first time since I entered. On the hill above us, the earth was literally covered with fragments of shell—Parrott, shrapnell, canister; besides lead in all shapes and forms, and a long kind of solid shot, shaped like a small Parrott shell. Minie balls lay in every direction, flattened, dented, and bent from the contact with trees and pieces of wood in their flight. The grass seemed deadened—the ground ploughed into furrows in many places; while scattered over all, like giants' pepper, in numberless quantity, were the shrapnell balls.

I could now see how very near to the rifle pits my cave lay: only a small ravine between the two hills separated us. In about two hours, General Bowen returned. No one knew, or seemed to know, why a truce had been made; but all believed that a treaty of surrender was pending. Nothing was talked about among the officers but the all-engrossing theme. Many wished to cut their way out and make the risk their own; but I secretly hoped that no such bloody hazard would be attempted.

The next morning, M— came up, with a pale face, saying: "It's all over! The white flag floats from our forts! Vicksburg has surrendered!"

He put on his uniform coat, silently buckled on his sword, and prepared to take out the men, to deliver up their arms in front of the fortification.

I felt a strange unrest, the quiet of the day was so unnatural. I walked up and down the cave until M— returned. The day was extremely warm; and he came with a violent headache. He told me that the Federal troops had acted splendidly; they were stationed opposite the place where the Confederate troops marched up and stacked their arms; and they seemed to feel sorry for the poor fellows who had defended the place for so long a time. Far different from what he had expected, not a jeer or taunt came from any one of the Federal soldiers. Occasionally, a cheer would be heard; but the majority seemed to regard the poor unsuccessful soldiers with a generous sympathy.

After the surrender, the old gray-headed soldier, in passing on the hill near the cave, stopped, and, touching his hat, said:

"It's a sad day this, madam; I little thought we'd come to it, when we first stopped in the intrenchments. I hope you'll yet be happy, madam, after all the trouble you've seen." . . .

SOURCE: *My Cave Life in Vicksburg*
(New York, 1864).

CHARLES MINOR BLACKFORD

As Confederate officer Charles Blackford records, Gettysburg, like the Civil War itself, began with Confederate triumph but ended in defeat.

LETTERS

June 25, 1863 [*Maryland, near Williamsport*] . . . The crossing the [Potomac] river by the troops was very picturesque. General Lee was on the bank on the Maryland side surrounded by ladies who came down to see the sight and to admire him. The soldiers waded into the water without stopping to roll up their pantaloons and came over in as good order as if on review, cheering at every step. One fellow, as he stepped on the Maryland shore, exclaimed, "Well, boys I've been seceding for two years and now I've got back into the Union again." Another said to a crowd of ladies, whom he supposed to be Union in their sentiments, "Here we are ladies, rough and ragged as ever, but back again to bother you."

The joy of the day was marred this evening by a military execution which took place in this division. I heard the death march, but fortunately did not hear the firing. It was not a victim of any trial in which I was judge-advocate, I am glad to say. . . .

June 26—1863. Greencastle, Penn. I crossed "Mason's and Dixon's line" to-day, and am now five or six miles within the boundaries of the Keystone State, surrounded by enemies and black looks, Dutchmen and big barns. Night before the last I slept on the "sacred soil," last night in "My Maryland," and to-night I will sweetly slumber in the land of Penn and protection. This is a very rapid change of venue for so large an army. . . . The people are greatly divided in sentiment, but the greater part are Unionists. The minority, however, is large and very enthusiastically Southern, and very bold in expressing their sentiments. . . . So far as I have seen, since crossing the Pennsylvania line, there is not much to indicate that we are in an enemy's country. The people, of course, are not pleased to see us, but they are not demonstrative in their hatred or very shy in their treatment of us. As no maltreatment is permitted, and no pillage other than that of their stock, they are so favorably disappointed they almost seem friendly. Private property is respected, and the men are not allowed even to go into a yard to get water without the permission of the owner. The orders even go so far, and they are very strictly enforced, as to prohibit our burning rails for firewood, a rule not enforced in Virginia and one I must say I think unnecessary here. Of course there will be some pillaging and even some violent robbery, for it is hard to strictly enforce any rule in so large an army, but such acts will be exceptional, as every possible means are taken to enforce General Lee's order, and the order meets the approval of the army. . . . .

July 3—Friday—1863.—Near Gettysburg. I left Chambersburg on yesterday morning at two o'clock and made a march of twenty-three miles by twelve o'clock, without a straggler, I believe. On the road we heard that the evening before (Wednesday, July 1,) General Lee had met the enemy about two miles from Gettysburg and had driven them back several miles, capturing some five thousand prisoners, without any serious loss on our part. Soon after we reached this place yesterday a very terrible battle begun, which raged until nine o'clock, the particulars of which I have not been able to gather, except that the two wings of the enemy were driven back with great loss, but their centre stood firm. We captured some two thousand, five hundred prisoners and, it is said, fifteen guns. All this, however, is but rumor, and even at corps headquarters we know little. . . . The fight commenced again this morning about four o'clock and has been raging at intervals and in different quarters ever since, until now, at ten o'clock, as I write under the shade of a tree, a terrible cannonading is going on. General Longstreet is a little to my right, awaiting orders, I suppose. His men are not yet engaged except the artillery. . . .

[*July*] *4—Saturday.* The battle [of Gettysburg] so increased in violence that I could no longer write. I knew it was a terrible battle, but how terrible I did not know until it was over. The results of the day even now are not accurately known. . . . I can only speak of what I saw. . . . They vastly outnumbered us, and though our men made a charge which will be the theme of the poet, the painter and the historian for all ages, they could not maintain the enemy's lines even when they captured them—the might of numbers will tell. Our loss in men and officers exceeds anything I have ever known. The loss is especially great among the officers, and those from Virginia particularly. . . .

SOURCE: *Memoirs of Life In and Out of the Army in
Virginia During the War Between the States*
(Lynchburg, Va., 1894–96).

JOHN MOSELEY

Three days of fighting at the Battle of Gettysburg yielded as many casualties as the number of Americans killed in the Vietnam War. General Lee lost a third of his army: 3,903 men were killed, 18,735 were wounded, and 5,425 were missing. On the Union side, 23,000 were killed, wounded, or missing, comprising almost one quarter of the federal troops. John Moseley, a Confederate soldier who fought at Gettysburg, wrote this final letter home to Alabama.

LETTER TO HIS MOTHER

Battlefield, Gettysburg Penn.
July 4, 1863

Dear Mother

I am here a prisoner of war & mortally wounded. I can live but a few hours more at farthest—I was shot fifty yards [from] the enemy's lines. They have been exceedingly kind to me.

I have no doubts as to the final results of this battle and I hope I may live long enough to hear the shouts of victory yet, before I die.

I am very weak. Do not mourn my loss. I had hoped to have been spared, but a righteous God has ordered it otherwise and I feel prepared to trust my case in his hands.

Farewell to you all. Pray that God may receive my soul.

Your unfortunate son John

SOURCE: *Soldiers Blue and Grey* by James L. Robertson, Jr.
Copyright 1988 by University of South Carolina Press.
Reprinted by permission.

DECIMUS ET ULTIMUS BARZIZA

Unlike many prisoners of war on both sides, Decimus et Ultimus Barziza of Louisiana had a relatively easy time of it. Wounded and captured at Gettysburg, he was treated in the hospital there before being sent to different prisons. This hospital stay gave him the opportunity to observe southerners and northerners side by side in the wake of the Battle of Gettysburg. Following his graphic views of battlefield surgery and soldiers' deaths, Barziza relates what he sees as the false cultural perceptions that northerners have of southerners and in so doing presents white southerners' perceptions of themselves. In this hall of mirrors, everything from behavior to terminology to ideas depends on the angle of vision.

from THE ADVENTURES OF A PRISONER OF WAR

In passing to the rear I saw the reinforcements of the enemy coming up, and was indeed somewhat surprised at the *nonchalance* they exhibited in marching steadily towards the firing.

I was taken to the Field Hospital of the Twelfth Army Corps, which had been established some distance in the rear of the lines. It consisted of the barn and other out-houses of a farm, sheds, &c., besides a great quantity of hospital tents, which were afterwards pitched.

About mid-day on Friday the battle of the 3d day opened heavily; the artillery was terrific; as it progressed, great anxiety was discernable among the Federals; the surgeons ceased their operations and looked anxiously to the front; hospital flags were perched on the fences, trees and houses; soon came streams of ammunition wagons, ambulances and disabled artillery, driving frantically to the rear; thousands of soldiers rushed back, and were driven up again to the front by cavalry in their rear; the wounded Federals, who were able to walk, were sent off hastily, and the scene was that of a routed and panic-stricken army. We, Confederates, who were at the hospital, were buoyant, and strained our eyes to see the grey backs rushing across the open field. But, alas! the storm gradually grew less violent, wavered, became more distant, and we knew the day was a bitter one for us. A little more vigor on the part of the Confederates that day would have secured the victory. Whilst the fight was raging this day, I was so confident that I remarked to the surgeon of the 12th corps, "Gen. Lee would have his Head Quarters by to-night ten miles on the Baltimore Pike." "It must be confessed," he replied, "that this looks somewhat like it." During all this day hundreds of wounded, both Confederate and Federal, were brought in. Our wounded were generally well treated, and were put side by side with the enemy's. Every shelter in the neighborhood was crammed; even hay-lofts were filled with the bleeding, mangled bodies. The surgeons, with sleeves rolled up and bloody to the elbows, were continually employed in amputating limbs. The red, human blood ran in streams from under the operating tables, and huge piles of arms and legs, withered and horrible to behold, were mute evidences of the fierceness of the strife.

He who has never seen the rear of an army during and immediately after a battle, can form no idea of the scene, while the mere mention of a Field Hospital to a soldier, brings up recollections of blood and brains, mangled limbs, protruding entrails, groans, shrieks and death. And when night comes upon them, and their wounds begin to grow chill, and pains shoot piercingly through them, then the deep and agonizing groans, the shrill death-shriek, the cries for water, opium, any thing, even death, make up the most horrible scene that can be conceived of. See that poor, bleeding boy turn his face to the surgeon and ask, "Doctor, is my wound mortal." And oh! what shades of agony, despair and dread flit across his features, as he hears the reply, "I fear it is, sir!" There lies one mortally wounded, sleeping "unto death," under the influence of opium, which has been given in large quantities to let him die easy. Now, one goes off in a convulsive spasm, another with a shriek, which causes the hair even of a hardened soldier to stand on end. And then the dead are laid out in long rows, with their naked faces turned up to the sun, their clothes stiff with the dried blood, and their features retaining in death the agony and pain which they died with; and presently they are dragged forth and thrust into a shallow pit, with, perhaps, the coarse jest of a vulgar soldier for their requiem, and bloody blankets for their winding sheets. What a blessing is it that the gentle and tender-loved ones at home are spared the sight of the last moments of their torn and mangled soldiers!

I could here but notice the exquisite order and arrangement of the Medical Department in the Federal army. Their ambulance corps is very numerous, and the supply of medicines is plentiful. Their surgeons assume a great deal of authority, and are feared and respected by the soldiers. Indeed, as might be expected from the material of their army, there is much distance kept up between officers and men; even their non-commissioned officers are ever mindful of the difference between themselves and the men.

I had opportunities for frequent conversation with the officers and soldiers, who seemed always eager for an argument. I was astonished to find what indifference prevailed amongst their soldiers in regard to the appointment and removal of their commanding Generals. Many of them did not know, nor did they seem to care who was in command of their army at this time. They all spoke well of Gen. Lee, and acknowledged him to be the "greatest Captain of the age." Many of them enquired whether it was true that Stonewall Jackson was really dead, or was it a story hatched up by their newspapers. I heard several express the belief that had Jackson been present, we would have won the battle, "for," said they, "he would have gotten lost and turned up some-where in our rear." On Saturday, the 4th, the wildest rumors were current. [Maj. Gen. George B.] McClellan was in Lee's rear with 150,000 militia, the Potomac had risen, Vicksburg had fallen, Charleston was ready to capitulate, and the Great Rebellion was crushed. Their loud cheering resounded along their lines, and great joy prevailed amongst them.

It happened that it rained the day before, and I, with many others, was put in a hay loft, and, there being no other means of reaching the ground save a ladder, I couldn't come down for several days, a situation I am sure I had not much relish for. When, however, I was able to come down, I chanced to stop before a tent a moment, when some wounded Massachusetts officers who occupied it invited me in, and we became quite social; more especially so as they were provided with some good liquor and cigars. I called to see them daily, but will not say which more attracted me, their conversation or their cheer. I was surprised at their assertion that our army was much better disciplined than theirs, and that was all the balance they would confess in our favor. Like all New Englanders, they were bigoted and full of vanity; they pretended to think the Massachusetts men made better soldiers than any others, and indulged in unbecoming sneers against Pennsylvanians, because they had not turned out *en masse* for the defense of their State. They were full of argument, and would listen to nothing but the Union. True types of their agitating and vain-glorious fathers of Plymouth Rock memory. I would usually answer their arguments by assuring them that, as they had inaugurated War, we accepted the issue, and artillery and musketry must decide the quarrel.

Some of these Yankees are really patriotic, and honestly or at least fanatically so. I was standing near an old man when word was brought him that his son had fallen a few hours before; he received the news with some apparent grief, and replied with much earnestness, "I wish I had fifty to fall for the same cause." Oh, Liberty! how many crimes are committed in thy name!

It is but justice to say that the chief Surgeon of the 12th Corps, Dr. McNulty, (I believe,) was very kind and attentive to our unfortunate people. This Field Hospital soon became very filthy, and the wounded were moved as fast as possible to Gettysburg. There was a college building in the town, which had been used by the Confederates whilst they occupied the place. To this building most of the Confederates were carried. The rooms and passages were densely crowded, and wounds of every shape and description afforded subjects for the attention of the humanitarians. There was a handsome yard adjoining the building, interspersed with shade trees. Thousands of citizens from all parts of the North flocked to Gettysburg to see a battle field and get a view of the terrible rebels. New England preachers, indellibly and unmistakably stamped with the hypocritical sanctity of Puritanism, stalked back and forth, with long faces and sanctimonious pretensions; they would occasionally come into a room and after sighing, and wheezing, and sucking their breath, would condescendingly give a poor rebel a tract and a cracker. Men and women, fresh from the very cess-pools of fanaticism and falsehood, would stand at the doors, and by their curious peering and simple questionings, gave much annoyance to our wounded. We always, however, had an infallible means at hand which would quickly cause their exodus, viz: we would ask them to give us money, clothing, or something to eat; we found this appeal to their charity would invariably rid us of their presence. But it is also just to state that many ladies showed much kindness to the "Rebels," but green Yankees never.

Whilst in Gettysburg, I could not but remark the difference between the conduct of our army and that of the enemy in invading our country. Here stood the town, after three days' hard fighting around and in it, almost entirely untouched. No wanton destruction of property of any description could be seen; no women and children complained that they were houseless and beggars. Then I called to mind the scenes around the city of Fredericsburg the winter previous; private houses sacked and burned, books, furniture, and every thing perishable utterly destroyed; women flying from burning houses with children in their arms, and insult and outrage at full license. I thought as I made the contrast in my own mind, of the utter uncongeniality of the two peoples, and thanked God that we were forever divided.

The Federals who came to visit us delighted to discuss the origin, cause and probable result of the Rebellion. There [sic] chief arguments were of the most puerile character. For instance, they dwelt with much satisfaction upon the fact that we fired the first gun at Sumpter, whose reverberations echoed and re-echoed through the whole extent of the North, and aroused a people to arms. I have often had occasion since to remark that this origin of the war is in the mouth of every man, woman and child who holds that their cause is just. The politicians have made this a potent physic, and the rabble eagerly swallowed it, as it was plain and undeniable, and could be understood and discussed by all without any further study or investigation. Oh! that horrible gun which has brought about so much mischief! They contended that States bore relation to the Federal Government, analagous to that which Counties bore to the State Government; the absurdity of which is so plain to any man who does not wish to be wrong. They also contended with much spirit that the new States formed since the establishment of the Government were the property of the United States, as they had been bought and paid for by Federal money. Such, then, were the main pretexts among the masses of the people of that country, for persisting in this most unrighteous crusade against the lives and liberties of independent States. But when all else failed, when every specious pretense was met, they relied defiantly upon that most miserable and destructive delusion, "The Union must be preserved." They pretended to believe that the Southern people were led blindfolded by their leaders, and were held down by the iron rule of force. They admitted that our soldiers were brave and fought with reckless daring, that our Generals were of the first order; but they always referred with confidence to their superiority of numbers, consoling themselves with the everlasting reflection that three men can, in time, conquer one. They declared they would never cease to war until we acknowledged the supremacy of the "best Government the world ever saw." They insisted that if we still continued to resist them, that our only fate must, in the nature of things, be extermination, and on us be the sin of it.

Verily, this is a peculiar people. They believe the United States Government holds a magic wand with which it can sway the nations of the earth at pleasure. They are extremely bigoted, and actually bloated with self-love. They think everything of their's [sic] is better than anybody else's; their religion purer; their men braver, and women fairer; their country better; their manners and customs more enlightened, and their intelligence and culture immeasurably superior. Brimfull of hypocritical cant and puritan ideas, they preach, pray and whine. The most parsimonious of wretches, they extol charity; the most inveterate blasphemers, they are the readiest exhorters; the worst of dastards, they are the most shameless boasters; the most selfish of men, they are the most blatant philanthropists; the blackesthearted hypocrites, they are religious fanatics. They are agitators and schemers, braggarts and deceivers, swindlers and extortioners, and yet pretend to godliness, truth, purity, and humanity. The shibboleth of their faith is, "the Union must and shall be preserved," and they hold on to this with all the obstinacy peculiar to their nature. They say we are a benighted people, and are trying to pull down that which God himself built up.

Many of these bigots expressed great astonishment at finding that the majority of our men could read and write; they have actually been educated to regard the Southern people as grossly illiterate, and as little better than savages. The whole nation lives, breathes and prospers in delusion; and their chiefs control the springs of the social and political machine with masterly hands.

I could but conclude that the Northern people were bent upon the destruction of the South. All appeared to deprecate the war, but were unwilling to listen to a separation of the old Union. They justified the acts of usurpation on the part of their Government, and seemed submissive to the tyranny of its acts on the plea of military necessity; they say the Union is better than the Constitution, and bow their necks to the yoke in the hope of success against us. A great many, I believe, act from honest and conscientious principle; many from fear and favor; but the large majority entertain a deep-seated hatred, envy and jealousy towards the Southern people and their institutions.

They know (yet they pretend not to believe it) that Southern men and women are their superiors in everything relating to bravery, honesty, virtue and refinement; and they have become more convinced of this since the present war; consequently, their worst passions have become aroused, and they give way to frenzy and fanaticism.

We must not deceive ourselves; they are bent upon our destruction, and differ mainly in the means of accomplishing this end.

However much as sections and parties they hate each other, yet, as a whole, they hate us more.

They are so entirely incongruous to our people, that they and their descendants will ever be our natural enemies.

But this digression, concerning the Yankee people, has carried me too far from the main subject of this work.

Some days elapsed before supplies sufficient for the wounded could be collected at Gettysburg. The whole hospital building and grounds soon became impregnated with the peculiar and sickening odor of blood and wounds.

We amused ourselves by rummaging over some books and papers that lay scattered about the rooms.

Soon, however, many ladies from Baltimore came to visit us, and spoke words of good cheer and encouragement.

I shall ever remember a gentleman from Baltimore, who came into the room where I was, and left me a bottle of fine brandy; it was a glorious treat, and right heartily was it enjoyed.

The wounded were removed as fast as possible from Gettysburg to Baltimore. Accordingly, some two hundred were put in box cars, on straw, and started.

Whilst at the depot we, of course, had many words with the citizens.

Whilst passing through the street, a Federal soldier ran up to our column and said, "Boys, if those fellows (meaning the guards) treat you badly, you must not think any thing of it, as they never smelt gunpowder."

At the depot a citizen was declaiming severely against the wicked rebellion, and predicting grand results from Federal arms, when one of our ragged soldiers placed his hand on his shoulder, and the following colloquy ensued:

Rebel. "Mister, do you belong to the army?"

Yank. "No sir, I do not—my cousin does."

Reb. "Mister, did you ever belong to the army?"

Yank. "No sir, why?"

Reb. "Because, Mister, when a man in my country talks as big as you do, he generally has on soldier's clothes, and a cartridge box belted around him. I would advise you to put on harness and trot to Gen. [Maj. Gen. George G.] Meade [Army of the Potomac]."

Yank. "Oh! you needn't give yourself any concern about Meade— he isn't sick; when it becomes necessary for me to go in the army, I am ready to go."

Reb. "Yes, I see you going, I'll bet a treat for the crowd you have just paid the three hundred dollar commutation. Your style don't like bullets; and a cock shouldn't crow if he is afraid to fight."

Yank. "You are very assuming, sir, for a man who is now dependent on us and our people for your very existence, and who is well taken care of by those you come to destroy. You have no rights, sir, save what the clemency of your enemies, for humanity sake, grants you."

Reb. (*Somewhat piqued.*) "I will let you know, sir, that I feel myself under no obligations to your Government for my good treatment. Whatever humanity may be shown us is forced from your Government. I am a soldier of the Confederate States, and my Government is able to demand proper treatment for its soldiers. We have plenty of Yankees down South, and it is this, and not humanity, which makes your Government clement, and deters you from putting in practice your declared outlawry against rebels."

The Yankee was about to reply, but was stopped by the guard. He went off shaking his head, and muttering something about the "confounded rebels."

After traveling all night, we arrived in Baltimore at day-break.

Ladies and children in numbers come crowding around the cars with refreshments, but were roughly and insultingly driven off by the guard.

For some reason we were compelled to lie in the cars all day until late in the evening.

Being provoked by the continued attempts of the ladies and boys to give us food and water, the officer of the guard had the hatches of the cars closed. Here, then, in a small box lay thirty helpless, bleeding men—their wounds very offensive and painful—almost suffocated, without a ray of light, and scarcely enough air to breathe. This piece of cruelty was continued for over half an hour, and when the hatches were again opened, we begged the ladies to go off, as they would kill us by this untold and wanton barbarity.

Crowds of men, women and children followed us towards the hospital.

We were in a sorry plight; our wounds had not been dressed for forty-eight hours; our clothes had never been changed since the battle—thus, bloody, dirty, ragged, bare-footed, bare-headed, and crippled, we marched through the streets of the monumental city, a spectacle of fiendish delight to some, but one of pity and sympathy to thousands of true subjugated Southerners, who inhabit this city.

Everything in the city of Baltimore gave evidence of the presence of oppression and tyranny. A Federal flag streamed from almost every window, and little miniature ones stuck upon the breasts of hundreds, as if they were worn as a talisman against insult and outrage. If a little girl dared wave her handkerchief at the Confederates, she was arrested or maltreated by the armed minions of despotism. Ladies, with baskets of provisions, followed tremblingly on the side-walks, and would be shaken roughly by the arm and insulted, if they approached us. Sympathy and pity shone upon the features of hundreds; and the sly look and troubled countenance showed plainly how they had been taught to fear the arms of their own Government. Baltimore is literally crushed and broken by high handed tyranny; the petty, ill-bred plebeians, with shoulder-straps on, actually lord it over these unfortunate people, with all the mean oppression which characterizes men of low estate who have been suddenly elevated to power. I saw at the West Building Hospital a lady arrested by a lubberly, bloated, and uncouth Hospital Steward, because she gave a white handkerchief to a wounded Confederate. Similar instances of mean and pitiful exhibitions of power are of daily occurrence. What a commentary upon the boasted freedom of the United States! May the proud Southern race disappear from the earth before they call these people masters!

Hundreds of our wounded were here collected and distributed to other places; some to David's Island, New York; others to Chester, Pennsylvania, and others to the various forts and prisons.

The Federals at this time were exceedingly jubilant. And, it must be confessed, that gloom was with the Confederates. Yet they were ever manly, impudent and independent.

From Baltimore I, with many others, was started on the cars for the hospital at Chester, Pennsylvania.

SOURCE: *The Adventures of a Prisoner of War; and Life and Scenes in Federal Prisons: Johnson's Island, Fort Delaware, and Point Lookout; by an Escaped Prisoner of Hood's Texas Brigade* (Houston, 1865). Reprinted by permission from the Center for American History, University of Texas at Austin.

MRS. STATTS

The loss of Union soldiers by March 1863 led Congress to pass a conscription act drafting 300,000 new troops over three years. Avoiding the draft was possible. A man could either enlist and collect a bounty or purchase a substitute for the high price of several hundred dollars. When the conscription law went into effect, riots by draft resisters broke out in several cities. Many white laborers blamed blacks for the war and feared their competition for jobs. In July, white resentment toward blacks sparked violence in New York City; three days of arson and street fighting left 119 dead and 306 wounded. Mrs. Statts describes her encounter with an angry white mob in New York City.

WM. HENRY NICHOLS*

. . . At 3 o'clock of that day the mob arrived and immediately commenced an attack with terrific yells, and a shower of stones and bricks, upon the house. In the next room to where I was sitting was a poor woman, who had been confined with a child on Sunday, three days previous. Some of the rioters broke through the front door with pick axes, and came rushing into the room where this poor woman lay, and commenced to pull the clothes from off her. Knowing that their rage was chiefly directed against men, I hid my son behind me and ran with him through the back door, down into the basement. In a little while I saw the innocent babe, of three days old, come crashing down into the yard; some of the rioters had dashed it out of the back window, killing it instantly. In a few minutes streams of water came pouring down into the basement, the mob had cut the Croton water-pipes with their axes. Fearing we should be drowned in the cellar, (there were ten of us, mostly women and children, there) I took my boy and flew past the dead body of the babe, out to the rear of the yard, hoping to escape with him through an open lot into 29th street; but here, to our horror and dismay, we met the mob again; I, with my son, had climbed the fence, but the sight of those maddened demons so affected me that I fell back, fainting, into the yard; my son jumped down from the fence to pick me up, and a dozen of the rioters came leaping over the fence after him. As they surrounded us my son exclaimed, "save my mother,

---

*William Henry Nichols was the son of the narrator, Mrs. Statts.

gentlemen, if you kill me." "Well, we will kill you," they answered; and with that two ruffians seized him, each taking hold of an arm, while a third, armed with a crow-bar, calling upon them to stand and hold his arms apart, deliberately struck him a heavy blow over the head, felling him, like a bullock, to the ground. (He died in the N.Y. hospital two days after). I believe if I were to live a hundred years I would never forget that scene, or cease to hear the horrid voices of that demoniacal mob resounding in my ears.

They then drove me over the fence, and as I was passing over, one of the mob seized a pocket-book, which he saw in my bosom, and in his eagerness to get it tore the dress off my shoulders.

I, with several others, then ran to the 29th street Station House, but we were here refused admittance, and told by the Captain that we were frightened without cause. A gentleman who accompanied us told the Captain of the facts, but we were all turned away.

SOURCE: *Report of the Committee of Merchants for the Relief of Colored People Suffering from the Late Riots in the City of New York* (New York, 1863). Reprinted by permission from the Schomburg Center for Research in Black Culture, New York Public Library. Astor, Lenox and Tilden Foundations.

HERMAN MELVILLE

Northern author Herman Melville had grave reservations at the best of times about the innate goodness of human nature. He thought that John Calvin's idea of the innate depravity of humanity was closer to the truth. The mob violence against black people in New York City served to confirm his belief.

THE HOUSE-TOP

A Night Piece.
(July 1863.)

No sleep. The sultriness pervades the air
And binds the brain—a dense oppression, such
As tawny tigers feel in matted shades.
Vexing their blood and making apt for ravage.
Beneath the stars the roofy desert spreads
Vacant as Libya. All is hushed near by.

Yet fitfully from far breaks a mixed surf
Of muffled sound, the Atheist roar of riot.
Yonder, where parching Sirius set in drought,
Balefully glares red Arson—there—and there.
The Town is taken by its rats—ship-rats
And rats of the wharves. All civil charms
And priestly spells which late held hearts in awe—
Fear-bound, subjected to a better sway
Than sway of self; these like a dream dissolve,
And man rebounds whole aeons back in nature.
Hail to the low dull rumble, dull and dead,
And ponderous drag that shakes the wall.
Wise Draco comes, deep in the midnight roll
Of black artillery; he comes, though late;
In code corroborating Calvin's creed
And cynic tyrannies of honest kings;
He comes, nor parlies; and the Town, redeemed,
Gives thanks devout; nor, being thankful, heeds
The grimy slur on the Republic's faith implied,
Which holds that Man is naturally good,
And—more—is Nature's Roman, never to be scourged.

SOURCE: *Battle-Pieces and Aspects of the War*
(New York, 1866).

LEWIS DOUGLASS

Comprised of one thousand black volunteers from Boston to Saint Louis, the Massachusetts 54th left for duty in May 1863. With limited knowledge of the terrain and in almost total darkness, this regiment led an attack on Fort Wagner, a battery located on Morris Island and a strategically important defense of the main shipping channel to Charleston, South Carolina. Shot and shell rained down heavily from the well-defended Confederate fort, inflicting heavy casualties on the federal forces and finally repulsing them. Yet the courage and tenacity of the Massachusetts 54th quieted doubts about the feasibility of blacks performing the duties of soldiers. While Frederick Douglass was fighting the political battle for civil rights in Washington, two of his sons were fighting with the all-black Massachusetts 54th on the coast of

South Carolina. One of them, Lewis Douglass, wrote this letter to his fiancée, Amelia Loguen, after attacking Fort Wagner.

LETTER TO AMELIA

Morris Island. S. C. July 20

My dear Amelia: I have been in two fights, and am unhurt. I am about to go in another I believe to-night. Our men fought well on both occasions. The last was desperate we charged that terrible battery on Morris Island known as Fort Wagoner, and were repulsed with a loss of 300 killed and wounded. I escaped unhurt from amidst that perfect hail of shot and shell. It was terrible. I need not particularize the papers will give a better than I have time to give. My thoughts are with you often, you are as dear as ever, be good enough to remember it as I no doubt you will. As I said before we are on the eve of another fight and I am very busy and have just snatched a moment to write you. I must necessarily be brief. Should I fall in the next fight killed or wounded I hope to fall with my face to the foe.

If I survive I shall write you a long letter. DeForrest of your city is wounded George Washington is missing, Jacob Carter is missing, Chas Reason wounded Chas Whiting, Chas Creamer all wounded. The above are in hospital.

This regiment has established its reputation as a fighting regiment not a man flinched, though it was a trying time. Men fell all around me. A shell would explode and clear a space of twenty feet, our men would close up again, but it was no use we had to retreat, which was a very hazardous undertaking. How I got out of that fight alive I can not tell, but I am here. My Dear girl I hope again to see you. I must bid you farewell should I be killed. Remember if I die I die in a good cause. I wish we had a hundred thousand colored troops we would put an end to this war. Good Bye to all Your own loving

Write soon   Lewis

SOURCE: Library of Congress,
Carter Woodson Papers,
1054.

HANNAH JOHNSON

In late 1862, Confederate President Jefferson Davis ordered that captured black soldiers be returned to the southern states to which they should belong and face

state-mandated punishments of enslavement or execution. White officers who were charged by the southerners with slave insurrection were also to be imprisoned or executed. Hannah Johnson's son was fighting with the 54th Massachusetts Infantry when she wrote to President Lincoln encouraging him to prevent this treatment of black soldiers.

LETTER TO MR. LINCOLN

Buffalo [N.Y.] July 31 1863

Excellent Sir

My good friend says I must write to you and she will send it My son went in the 54th regiment. I am a colored woman and my son was strong and able as any to fight for his country and the colored people have as much to fight for as any. My father was a Slave and escaped from Louisiana before I was born morn forty years agone I have but poor edication but I never went to schol, but I know just as well as any what is right between man and man. Now I know it is right that a colored man should go and fight for his country, and so ought to a white man. I know that a colored man ought to run no greater risques than a white, his pay is no greater his obligation to fight is the same. So why should not our enemies be compelled to treat him the same, Made to do it.

My son fought at Fort Wagoner but thank God he was not taken prisoner, as many were I thought of this thing before I let my boy go but then they said Mr. Lincoln will never let them sell our colored soldiers for slaves, if they do he will get them back quick he will rettally-ate and stop it. Now Mr. Lincoln dont you think you oght to stop this thing and make them do the same by the colored men they have lived in idleness all their lives on stolen labor and made savages of the colored people, but they now are so furious because they are proving themselves to be men, such as have come away and got some edication. It must not be so. You must put the rebels to work in State prisons to making shoes and things, if they sell our colored soldiers, till they let them all go. And give their wounded the same treatment. it would seem cruel, but their no other way, and a just man must do hard things sometimes, that shew him to be a great man. They tell me some do you will take back the Proclamation, don't do it. When you are dead and in Heaven, in a thousand years that action of yours will make the

Angels sing your praises I know it. Ought one man to own another, law for or not, who made the law, surely the poor slave did not. so it is wicked, and a horrible Outrage, there is no sense in it, because a man has lived by robbing all his life and his father before him, should he complain because the stolen things found on him are taken. Robbing the colored people of their labor is but a small part of the robbery their souls are almost taken, they are made bruits of often. You know all about this

Will you see that the colored men fighting now, are fairly treated. You ought to do this, and do it at once, Not let the thing run along meet it quickly and manfully, and stop this, mean cowardly cruelty. We poor oppressed ones, appeal to you, and ask fair play.

Yours for Christs sake
Hannah Johnson

SOURCE: National Archives, J-17 1863,
Letters Received, ser. 360,
Colored Troops Division,
RG 94 [B-34].

CORPORAL JAMES HENRY GOODING

The black soldiers who served in the Union army and navy numbered 208,943, filling the ranks of 166 segregated regiments. Initially, they received lower wages as well as disdainful treatment from the white troops. James Henry Gooding, a black corporal from Massachusetts, filed this grievance with President Lincoln on the unequal pay scale for black soldiers.

LETTER TO MR. LINCOLN

Camp of 54th Mass Colored Regt

Morris Island Dept of the South, Sept. 28th 1863.

Your Excelency Abraham Lincoln:

Your Excelency will pardon the presumtion of an humble individual like myself, in addressing you. but the earnest Solicitation of my Comrades in Arms, besides the genuine interest felt by myself in the matter is my excuse, for placing before the Executive head of the Nation our Common Grievance: On the 6th of the last Month, the Paymaster of the department, informed us, that if we would decide to recieve the sum of $10 (ten dollars) per month, he would come and pay us that sum, but, that, on the sitting of Congress, the Regt would, in his opinion, be *allowed* the other 3 (three.) He did not give us any guarantee that this would be, as he hoped, certainly *he* had no authority for making any such guarantee, and we can not supose him acting in any way interested. Now the main question is. Are we *Soldiers*, or are we LABOURERS. We are fully armed, and equipped, have done all the various Duties, pertaining to a Soldiers life, have conducted ourselves, to the complete satisfaction of General Officers, who, were if any, prejudiced *against* us, but who now accord us all the encouragement, and honour due us: have shared the perils, and Labour, of Reducing the first stronghold, that flaunted a Traitor Flag: and more, Mr President. Today, the Anglo Saxon Mother, Wife, or Sister, are not alone, in tears for departed Sons, Husbands, and Brothers. The patient Trusting Decendants of Africs Clime, have dyed the ground with blood, in defense of the Union, and Democracy. Men too your Excellency, who know in a measure, the cruelties of the Iron heel of oppression, which in years gone by, the very Power, their blood is now being spilled to maintain, ever ground them to the dust. But When the war trumpet sounded o'er the land, when men knew not the Friend from the Traitor, the Black man laid his life at the Altar of the Nation,—and he was refused. When the arms of the Union, were beaten, in the first year of the War, And the Executive called more food for its ravaging maw, again the black man begged, the privelege of Aiding his Country in her need, to be again refused, And now, he is in the War: and how has he conducted himself? Let their dusky forms, rise up, out the mires of James Island, and give the answer. Let the rich mould around Wagners parapets be upturned, and there will be found an Eloquent answer. Obedient and patient, and Solid as a wall are they. . . . Now Your Excellency, We have done a Soldiers Duty. Why cant we have a Soldiers pay? You caution the Rebel Chieftain, that the United States, knows, no distinction, in her Soldiers: She insists on having all her Soldiers, of whatever, creed or Color, to be treated, according to the usages of War. Now if the United States exacts uniformity of treatment of her Soldiers, from the Insurgents, would it not be well, and consistent, to set the example herself, by paying all her *Soldiers* alike? We of this Regt. were not enlisted under any "contraband" act. But we do wish to be understood, as rating our Service, of more Value to the Government, than the service of the exslave, Their Service *is* undoubtedly worth much to the Nation, but Congress made express, provision touching their case, as slaves freed by military necessity, and assuming the Government, to be their temporary Gaurdian:—Not so with us—Freemen by birth, and consequently, having the advantage of *thinking*, and acting for ourselves, so far as the Laws would allow us. We do not consider ourselves fit subjects for the Contraband act. We appeal to You, Sir: as the Executive of the Nation, to have us Justly Dealt with. The Regt, do pray, that they be assured their service will be fairly appreciated, by paying them as american SOLDIERS, not as menial hierlings. . . . If you, as chief Magistrate of the Nation, will assure us, of our whole pay. We are content, our Patriotism, our enthusiasm will have a new impetus, to exert our energy more and more to aid Our Country. Not that our hearts ever flagged, in Devotion, spite the evident apathy displayed in our behalf, but We feel as though, our Country spurned us, now we are sworn to serve her.

Please give this a moments attention.

Corporal James Henry Gooding
Co. C. 54th Mass. Regt
Morris Island S.C.

SOURCE: National Archives, 28 Sept. 1863
enclosed in [Harper & Brothers] to
[Abraham Lincoln], 12 Oct. 1863,
H-133, 1863 Letters Received,
ser. 360, Colored Troops Division,
RG 94 [B-408].

SARAH EMMA EDMONDS

For over two years Sarah Emma E. Edmonds worked as a Union spy and field and hospital nurse, serving through major battles of the First and Second Bull Run and the Battle of Fredericksburg. These excerpts from her diary include a few examples of her unconventional escapades.

from NURSE AND SPY IN THE UNION ARMY

. . . The third day after my arrival I went out with a reconnoitering expedition, under command of General M. It was entirely composed of cavalry. We rode thirty-six miles that afternoon—the roads were splendid. When we were about twelve miles from our lines we changed our course and struck through the woods, fording creeks and crossing swamps, which was anything but pleasant.

After emerging from the thick undergrowth, on one occasion, we came upon an inferior force of the enemy's cavalry; a sharp skirmish ensued, which resulted in the capture of five prisoners from the rebel band, and wounding several. Three of our men were slightly wounded, but we returned to Louisville in good order, and enjoyed the luxury of a good supper at a hotel, which is a rare thing in that city.

I took the cars the next day and went to Lebanon—dressed in one of the rebel prisoner's clothes—and thus disguised, made another trip to rebeldom. My business purported to be buying up butter and eggs, at the farm-houses, for the rebel army. I passed through the lines somewhere, without knowing it; for on coming to a little village toward evening, I found it occupied by a strong force of rebel cavalry. The first house I went to was filled with officers and citizens. I had stumbled upon a wedding party, unawares. Captain Logan, a recruiting officer, had been married that afternoon to a brilliant young widow whose husband had been killed in the rebel army a few months before. She had discovered that widow's weeds were not becoming to her style of beauty, so had decided to appear once more in bridal costume, for a change.

I was questioned pretty sharply by the handsome captain in regard to the nature of my business in that locality, but finding me an innocent, straightforward Kentuckian, he came to the conclusion that I was all right. But he also arrived at the conclusion that I was old enough to be in the army, and bantered me considerably upon my want of patriotism.

The rebel soldier's clothes which I wore did not indicate any thing more than that I was a Kentuckian—for their cavalry do not dress in any particular uniform, for scarcely two of them dress alike—the only uniformity being that they most generally dress in butternut color.

I tried to make my escape from that village as soon as possible, but just as I was beginning to congratulate myself upon my good fortune, who should confront me but Captain Logan. Said he: "See here, my lad; I think the best thing you can do is to enlist, and join a company which is just forming here in the village, and will leave in the morning. We are giving a bounty to all who freely enlist, and are conscripting those who refuse. Which do you propose to do, enlist and get the bounty, or refuse, and be obliged to go without anything?" I replied, "I think I shall wait a few days before I decide." "But we can't wait for you to decide," said the captain; "the Yankees may be upon us any moment, for we are not far from their lines, and we will leave here either tonight or in the morning early. I will give you two hours to decide this

question, and in the mean time you must be put under guard." So saying, he marched me back with him, and gave me in charge of the
guards. In two or three hours he came for my decision, and I told him
that I had concluded to wait until I was conscripted. "Well," said he,
"you will not have long to wait for that, so you may consider yourself
a soldier of the Confederacy from this hour, and subject to military
discipline."

This seemed to me like pretty serious business, especially as I
would be required to take the oath of allegiance to the Confederate
Government. However, I did not despair, but trusted in Providence and
my own ingenuity to escape from this dilemma also; and as I was not
required to take the oath until the company was filled up, I was determined to be among the missing ere it became necessary for me to
make any professions of loyalty to the rebel cause. I knew that if I
should refuse to be sworn into the service after I was conscripted, that
in all probability my true character would be suspected, and I would
have to suffer the penalty of death—and that, too, in the most barbarous manner.

I was glad to find that it was a company of cavalry that was being
organized, for if I could once get on a good horse there would be some
hope of my escape. There was no time to be lost, as the captain remarked, for the Yankees might make a dash upon us at any moment;
consequently a horse and saddle was furnished me, and everything
was made ready for a start immediately. Ten o'clock came, and we had
not yet started. The captain finally concluded that, as everything
seemed quiet, we would not start until daylight.

Music and dancing was kept up all night, and it was some time
after daylight when the captain made his appearance. A few moments
more and we were trotting briskly over the country, the captain com-
plimenting me upon my horsemanship, and telling me how grateful I
would be to him when the war was over and the South had gained her
independence, and that I would be proud that I had been one of the
soldiers of the Southern confederacy, who had steeped my saber in
Yankee blood, and driven the vandals from our soil. "Then," said he,
"you will thank me for the interest which I have taken in you, and for
the *gentle persuasives* which I made use of to stir up your patriotism
and remind you of your duty to your country."

In this manner we had traveled about half an hour, when we suddenly encountered a reconnoitering party of the Federals, cavalry in
advance, and infantry in the rear. A contest soon commenced; we were
ordered to advance in line, which we did, until we came within a few
yards of the Yankees.

The company advanced, but my horse suddenly became unmanageable, and it required a second or two to bring him right again; and before I could overtake the company and get in line the contending parties had met in a hand to hand fight.

All were engaged, so that when I, by accident, got on the Federal side of the line, none observed me for several minutes, except the Federal officer, who had recognized me and signed to me to fall in next to him. That brought me face to face with my rebel captain, to whom I owed such a debt of gratitude. Thinking this would be a good time to cancel all obligations in that direction, I discharged the contents of my pistol in his face.

This act made me the center of attraction. Every rebel seemed determined to have the pleasure of killing me first, and a simultaneous dash was made toward me and numerous saber strokes aimed at my head. Our men with one accord rushed between me and the enemy, and warded off the blows with their sabers, and attacked them with such fury that they were driven back several rods.

The infantry now came up and deployed as skirmishers, and succeeded in getting a position where they had a complete cross-fire on the rebels, and poured in volley after volley until nearly half their number lay upon the ground. Finding it useless to fight longer at such a disadvantage they turned and fled, leaving behind them eleven killed, twenty-nine wounded, and seventeen prisoners.

The confederate captain was wounded badly but not mortally; his handsome face was very much disfigured, a part of his nose and nearly half of his upper lip being shot away. I was sorry, for the graceful curve of his mustache was sadly spoiled, and the happy bride of the previous morning would no longer rejoice in the beauty of that manly face and exquisite mustache of which she seemed so proud, and which had captivated her heart ere she had been three months a widow.

Our men suffered considerable loss before the infantry came up, but afterward scarcely lost a man. I escaped without receiving a scratch, but my horse was badly cut across the neck with a saber, but which did not injure him materially, only for a short time.

After burying the dead, Federal and rebel, we returned to camp with our prisoners and wounded, and I rejoiced at having once more escaped from the confederate lines.

I was highly commended by the commanding general for my coolness throughout the whole affair, and was told kindly and candidly that I would not be permitted to go out again in that vicinity, in the capacity of spy, as I would most assuredly meet with some of those who had seen me desert their ranks, and I would consequently be hung up to the nearest tree.

Not having any particular fancy for such an exalted position, and not at all ambitious of having my name handed down to posterity among the list of those who "expiated their crimes upon the gallows," I turned my attention to more quiet and less dangerous duties.

SOURCE: *Nurse and Spy in the Union Army*
(Hartford, 1865).

SARAH J. WOODSON

Education had long been a priority for blacks in the North. That tradition was accelerated with the increased migration from the South after the Emancipation Proclamation. Sarah J. Woodson graduated from Oberlin College in 1856 and taught in Ohio's black schools. In this 1863 speech to the Ohio Colored Teachers Association, she enunciates the values and goals of black education in the new world coming to life in the middle of the war's carnage and destruction.

ADDRESS TO THE YOUTH

. . . If you take a retrospect of the past, you perceive that in the darkest periods, when truth and virtue appeared to sleep, when science had dropped her telescope and philosophy its torch, when the world would have seemed to be standing still, the inscrutable wisdom of Divine Providence was preparing new agents, and evolving new principles, to aid in the work of individual and social improvement.

It would appear as if the world, like the year, had its seasons; and that the seed disseminated in spring time, must first die before it can vegetate and produce the rich harvests of autumn. The developments of one period seem obscured for a season, by the unfolding of the great mysterious curtain, by which to disclose the glories of the next.

History has marked to us such periods, and we are disheartened by the necessary and successive seasons of darkness, because the revolution is so great, or, our own position so humble, that we cannot look beyond the shade that surrounds us, and behold the distant but gradual approach of a better day. Though for a season darkness has covered the land, and gross darkness the people, and the energies of our people have been stultified by the accumulated prejudices of generations, which have been heaped upon us, yet there is reason to be encouraged. . . .

Yes, the sombre clouds of ignorance and superstition which so long enshrouded us and seemed ready to close upon us, as the funeral pall of our national existence, is being dispersed before the light of eternal truth. The sign of promise, the great precursor of a brighter day, has already enlightened the long night of our oppression, and the broad sun of our liberty begins to illuminate our political horizon. The mighty empire of despotism and oppression is trembling to its foundation, it must soon crumble and fall; but will we submit to sink and be buried beneath its ruins? Will we alone be quiescent and passive, while all around us is agitation and progress?

Do the revolutions which surround us awaken in our souls no desire to partake of the onward movement? The world moves right on, and he who moves not with it, must be crushed beneath its revolving wheels. You stand on the eve of a brighter day than has ever enlightened your pathway. The obstacles which have so long barred you from the portals of knowledge, are fast being removed, and the temple of science from which you have hitherto been ousted with tenacious jealousy, will soon disclose to you the glory of his inner sanctuary. Wisdom, with a friendly hand, beckons you to enter and revel in her courts. . . .

Apply your minds, then, early and vigorously to those studies which will not only endow you with the power and privilege to walk abroad, interested spectators of all that is magnificent and beautiful, above and around you, but to commune with that which is illustrious in the records of the past, and noble and divine in the development of the future.

Would you be eminent among your fellow-mortals, and have your name inscribed on the pages of history, as a living representative of truth, morality and virtue? Would you, by deeds of heroism and noble achievements, vie with the proud sons of honor, and share with them the immortal wreath which the hand of time has placed upon their brow? Would you ascend the hill of science, and there contend with their votaries for the laurels plucked from its fair summit? Would you penetrate the secret labyrinths of the universe, and gather from their hoarded mysteries that knowledge which will bless generations to come? Then apply your minds to study, profound, intricate study. Let your time, your money, your interest all be spent in the pursuit of this one great object, the improvement of your mind. It is only from the deepest furrows that the richest harvests are gathered. The breathings of genius are not produced "ad libitum." The lyres of the soul bring no sound to the touch of unpracticed hands. So the creative powers of the mind are never developed till drawn forth by the deep, harrowing process of education. Oh, there are wells of inspiration in every human heart, from which angels might draw, and leave them unexhausted. Fathom the depths of your nature, draw from its profound resources those principles which will ennoble and strengthen your intellectual powers. Educate the youth of the present, and our nation will produce a constellation of glowing minds, whose light will brighten the path of generations to come. Hitherto there has scarcely been a mind among us, which has sent forth a spark into the vast region of science. The arts have received but little attention, and literature has found no place among us. Yet, by the efforts which may be put forth by the present generation, the arts, science and literature may be as widely diffused among us, and we may become as eminent, in point of intellectual attainments, as any people who have had an existence.

We call upon you to accept the means which God has placed in your power. The great and the good, and the noble, who have preceded you, and have bequeathed to you the hoarded treasures of their richly cultivated minds, call upon you. The voice of millions, who are perishing without a ray of intellectual light, call upon you. Everything above and around you combine to stimulate you to the work of removing darkness and error, and establishing truth and virtue. And may God speed the work, till science, philosophy and religion, the great elevators of fallen humanity, shall have completed the work of moral refinement, and we in the enjoyment of all our rights, both political and civil, will stand at the summit of national glory.

SOURCE: *The Semi-Centenary and the Retrospection of the African Methodist Episcopal Church,* edited by Daniel A. Payne (Baltimore, 1866).

J. W. LINDSAY

For black Americans in the process of liberating themselves from the institution of slavery before and during the Civil War, Canada appeared to be the promised land. J. W. Lindsay was a freeborn black child who was kidnapped and taken to Tennessee. As a young man, he and a friend decided to escape. To avoid kidnapping in the North again, they kept going until they got to Toronto. What Lindsay found in Canada he describes here during testimony before the American Freedman's Inquiry Commission.

TESTIMONY

St. Catharines, Nov. 6th 1863

. . . I find the prejudice here the same as in the States. I don't find any difference at all. In fact, as far as prejudice goes, the slaveholders have not so much absolute prejudice as the people here—not half. In this country, they will twit us with having been in Virginia, and about having been in slavery. They take hold of it as a handle to throw their stigmas upon us. We may have the best teams in the world, & the best means in the world to carry on business, but unless we can make business within ourselves, such as gardening or something of that kind, we cannot get anything to do. Here are our children, that we think as much of as white people think of theirs, and want them elevated and educated; but, although I have been here thirty years, I have never seen a scholar made here amongst the colored people. I speak only of St. Catharines. There are several graduates in Toronto, I know. The Irish are getting so, down at the docks, where the colored men may do a few hours' work, once in a while, loading & unloading, that they want to run them off the docks. Then here are two railroads, & here is the canal, where there are about 300 hands employed, and you won't see a colored face at either of them. The white folks won't give them any chance at all. I have asked the authorities here—"What are you going to do with the colored people? What will become of them? What kind of citizens will they make? You will only make paupers & culprits of them." They set a side school off for the colored children, and gathered them up from one end of the town to the other. They have had an old drunken teacher for several years, who has been killing time, not half teaching the children—sometimes lying drunk in the school house, it is said, and the children playing on the outside. My children are as much advanced, just by what they can spell out at home, as children that go there. . . .

We feel the effects of slavery desperately in this country. Slavery curses every man on the continent of America. Very often, when a colored man goes to a farmer for work, he will not take him, though he may want help ever so bad, because he won't condescend to have him about his house. Maybe his wife will say, "I am not going to the trouble of setting two tables," and so the poor fellow has to go and get his living the best way he can. All this is the effect of slavery. . . .

The war affects us badly here. It deranges money matters, and when the white people come to hunt up the foundation of it, they say it is on account of the "niggers." There is not a farmer here who will take U.S. money now, any more than he will touch poison, where as, it used to be current here like our own money. Of course, there are many things that would draw U.S. money into the country, if it would only pass. There is a great deal of prejudice here, because there are a good many Americans here. We should find more substantial friends in Georgia or South Carolina, who would really do us a kindness; than we should find here. I found the people in Pittsburg, Pa., very familiar; and in fact, so far as treatment, & the rights of humanity and hospitality are concerned, I never saw any place where I enjoyed myself so much as in Pittsburg. There are a great many Englishmen who come to this country, and they seem, when they first came here, quite moderate in their views. They do not seem to have so much scorn of the black man, nor so much disposition to browbeat him, as the Canadians, because it is not tolerated in England. The black man is thought a great deal of there. We had an Englishman to preach for us in our church a couple of weeks ago, who had not been out from England but a little while, and he said he was really surprised when he came to America to see how isolated and browbeaten the colored people were. In fact, I have seen so much of prejudice, and its dirty work, that I have absolutely come to the conclusion that it is wicked in the first degree; that it is a wicked outrage upon the human family; that those who cherish it are blaming the Almighty Creator of all things. . . .

SOURCE: National Archives, American Freedman's Inquiry Commission, Canadian Testimony filed with 0-328-1863, RG 94 [M-619].

HENRY TIMROD

Henry Timrod served simultaneously as a member of the Confederate army and as a correspondent for the Charleston Mercury *until, like so many soldiers on both sides, he contracted tuberculosis. He returned home to live through General Sherman's burning of South Carolina cities and through near starvation until he succumbed to tuberculosis in 1867. Called by many the poet laureate of the Confederacy, Timrod distilled in a small literary work the essence of southern pride and suffering.*

SPRING

Spring, with that nameless pathos in the air
Which dwells with all things fair,
Spring, with her golden suns and silver rain,
Is with us once again.

Out in the lonely woods the jasmine burns
Its fragrant lamps, and turns
Into a royal court with green festoons
The banks of dark lagoons.

In the deep heart of every forest tree
The blood is all aglee,
And there's a look about the leafless bowers
As if they dreamed of flowers.

Yet still on every side we trace the hand
Of Winter in the land,
Save where the maple reddens on the lawn,
Flushed by the season's dawn;

Or where, like those strange semblances we find
That age to childhood bind,
The elm puts on, as if in Nature's scorn,
The brown of Autumn corn.

As yet the turf is dark, although you know
That, not a span below,
A thousand germs are groping through the gloom,
And soon will burst their tomb.

Already, here and there, on frailest stems
Appear some azure gems,
Small as might deck, upon a gala day,
The forehead of a fay.

In gardens you may note amid the dearth
The crocus breaking earth;
And near the snowdrop's tender white and green,
The violet in its screen.

But many gleams and shadows need must pass
Along the budding grass,
And weeks go by, before the enamored South
Shall kiss the rose's mouth.

Still there's a sense of blossoms yet unborn
In the sweet airs of morn;
One almost looks to see the very street
Grow purple at his feet.

At times a fragrant breeze comes floating by,
And brings, you know not why,
A feeling as when eager crowds await
Before a palace gate

Some wondrous pageant: and you scarce would start,
If from a beech's heart,
A blue-eyed Dryad, stepping forth, should say,
"Behold me! I am May!"

Ah! who would couple thoughts of war and crime
With such a blessed time!
Who in the west wind's aromatic breath
Could hear the call of Death!

Yet not more surely shall the Spring awake
The voice of wood and brake,
Than she shall rouse, for all her tranquil charms,
A million men to arms.

There shall be deeper hues upon her plains
Than all her sunlit rains,
And every gladdening influence around,
Can summon from the ground.

Oh! standing on this desecrated mould,
Methinks that I behold,
Lifting her bloody daisies up to God,
Spring kneeling on the sod,

And calling, with the voice of all her rills,
Upon the ancient hills
To fall and crush the tyrants and the slaves
Who turn her meads to graves.

THE UNKNOWN DEAD

The rain is plashing on my sill,
But all the winds of Heaven are still;
And so it falls with that dull sound
Which thrills us in the church-yard ground,
When the first spadeful drops like lead
Upon the coffin of the dead.

Beyond my streaming window-pane,
I cannot see the neighboring vane,
Yet from its old familiar tower
The bell comes, muffled, through the shower.
What strange and unsuspected link
Of feeling touched, has made me think—
While with a vacant soul and eye
I watch the gray and stony sky—
Of nameless graves on battle-plains
Washed by a single winter's rains,
Where, some beneath Virginian hills,
And some by green Atlantic rills,
Some by the waters of the West,
A myriad unknown heroes rest.
Ah! not the chiefs, who, dying, see
Their flags in front of victory,
Or, at their life-blood's noble cost
Pay for a battle nobly lost,
Claim from their monumental beds
The bitterest tears a nation sheds.
Beneath yon lonely mound—the spot
By all save some fond few forgot—
Lie the true martyrs of the fight
Which strikes for freedom and for right.
Of them, their patriot zeal and pride,
The lofty faith that with them died,
No grateful page shall farther tell
Than that so many bravely fell;
And we can only dimly guess
What worlds of all this world's distress,
What utter woe, despair, and dearth,
Their fate has brought to many a hearth.
Just such a sky as this should weep
Above them, always, where they sleep;
Yet, haply, at this very hour,
Their graves are like a lover's bower;
And Nature's self, with eyes unwet,
Oblivious of the crimson debt
To which she owes her April grace,
Laughs gayly o'er their burial-place.

SOURCE: *War Poetry of the South,*
edited by William Gilmore Simms
(New York, 1867).

ABRAHAM LINCOLN

The thousands of corpses from Gettysburg were buried in the new Gettysburg National Cemetery. On November 19, 1863, President Lincoln dedicated the burial ground in a brief address that revitalizes the core concepts of the Declaration of Independence, making liberty and equality central to the American identity.

GETTYSBURG ADDRESS

Fourscore and seven years ago our fathers brought forth upon this continent a new nation, conceived in liberty, and dedicated to the proposition that all men are created equal. Now we are engaged in a great civil war, testing whether that nation, or any nation so conceived and so dedicated, can long endure. We are met on a great battle-field of that war. We have come to dedicate a portion of that field as a final resting-place for those who here gave their lives that that nation might live. It is altogether fitting and proper that we should do this. But in a larger sense we cannot dedicate, we cannot consecrate, we cannot hallow this ground. The brave men, living and dead, who struggled here, have consecrated it far above our power to add or detract. The world will little note, nor long remember, what we say here, but it can never forget what they did here. It is for us, the living, rather to be dedicated here to the unfinished work which they who fought here have thus far so nobly advanced. It is rather for us to be here dedicated to the great task remaining before us, that from these honored dead we take increased devotion to that cause for which they gave the last full measure of devotion; that we here highly resolve that these dead shall not have died in vain; that this nation, under God, shall have a new birth of freedom, and that government of the people, by the people, and for the people, shall not perish from the earth.

SOURCE: *The Life and Public Services of Abraham Lincoln* by Henry J. Raymond (New York, 1865).

SECTION 4 1864–1865

In March 1864, the newly reelected President Lincoln appointed Ulysses S. Grant commander-in-chief of the Union army. Organizing a focused campaign, Grant traveled south to meet Lee and his Army of Northern Virginia, and sent General William Sherman from the west into Georgia. General Sherman's army captured Atlanta, moved through Georgia to the sea, and then headed toward the Carolinas leaving widespread destruction and welcoming liberated slaves into its ranks along the way. By the winter of 1865, this military strategy against an enemy declining in morale, lacking supplies, and suffering high rates of desertion produced a sense of doom in the South.

In April 1865, federal troops took Richmond. When the southern troops retreated, the Confederate government evacuated the city, setting fire to several buildings as they fled. The Union was restored when General Lee surrendered to General Grant at Appomattox Court House on April 9, 1865. Five days later, President Lincoln was assassinated. On December 18, 1865 the Thirteenth Amendment to the Constitution was ratified, abolishing slavery throughout the United States.

These selections highlight the strengths that men and women, white and black, in the military or in civilian life, exhibited as they endured the cruelties, injustices, and costly triumphs of the final war years.

Sarah Morgan Dawson

Sarah Morgan Dawson, the young Confederate woman from New Orleans, dramatizes her family's response to news of the deaths of two of their own. Moving emotionally among denial, anger, and acceptance of the will of God, she reenacts in her diary an experience common to the home front in all wars.

FEBRUARY 5

5th.

Not dead! not dead! O my God! Gibbes is *not* dead! Where—O dear God! Another?

Only a few days ago came a letter so cheerful and hopeful—we have waited and prayed so patiently—at my feet lies one from Colonel Steadman saying he is dead. Dead! Suddenly and without a moment's warning summoned to God! No! it cannot be! I am mad! O God, have mercy on us! My poor mother! And Lydia! Lydia! God comfort you! My brain seems afire. Am I mad? Not yet! God would not take him yet! He will come again! Hush, God is good! Not dead! not dead!

O Gibbes, come back to us!

FEBRUARY 11

11th.

O God, O God, have mercy on us! George is dead! Both in a week. George, our sole hope—our sole dependence.

MARCH

March.

Dead! Dead! Both dead! O my brothers! What have we lived for except you? We, who would have so gladly laid down our lives for yours, are left desolate to mourn over all we loved and hoped for, weak and helpless; while you, so strong, noble, and brave, have gone before us without a murmur. God knows best. But it is hard—O so hard! to give them up. . . .

If we had had any warning or preparation, this would not have been so unspeakably awful. But to shut one's eyes to all dangers and risks, and drown every rising fear with "God will send them back; I will not doubt His mercy," and then suddenly to learn that your faith has been presumption—and God wills that you shall undergo bitter affliction—it is a fearful awakening! What glory have we ever rendered to God that we should expect him to be so merciful to us? Are not all things His, and is not He infinitely more tender and compassionate than we deserve?

We have deceived ourselves wilfully about both. After the first dismay on hearing of Gibbes's capture, we readily listened to the assertions of our friends that Johnson's Island was the healthiest place in the world; that he would be better off, comfortably clothed and under shelter, than exposed to shot and shell, half fed, and lying on the bare ground during Ewell's winter campaign. We were thankful for his safety, knowing Brother would leave nothing undone that could add to his comfort. And besides that, there was the sure hope of his having him paroled. On that hope we lived all winter—now confident that in a little while he would be with us, then again doubting for a while, only to have the hope grow surer afterwards. And so we waited and prayed, never doubting he would come at last. He himself believed it, though striving not to be too hopeful lest he should disappoint us, as well as himself. Yet he wrote cheerfully and bravely to the last. Towards the middle of January, Brother was sure of succeeding, as all the prisoners had been placed under Butler's control. Ah me! How could we be so blind? We were sure he would be with us in a few weeks! I wrote to him that I had prepared his room.

On the 30th of January came his last letter, addressed to me, though meant for Lavinia. It was dated the 12th—the day George died. All his letters pleaded that I would write more frequently—he loved to hear from me; so I had been writing to him every ten days. On the 3d of February I sent my last. Friday the 5th, as I was running through Miriam's room, I saw Brother pass the door, and heard him ask Miriam for mother. The voice, the bowed head, the look of utter despair on his face, struck through me like a knife. "Gibbes! Gibbes!" was my sole thought; but Miriam and I stood motionless looking at each other without a word. "Gibbes is dead," said mother as he stood before her. He did not speak; and then we went in.

We did not ask how, or when. That he was dead was enough for us. But after a while he told us Uncle James had written that he had died at two o'clock on Thursday the 21st. Still we did not know how he had died. Several letters that had been brought remained unopened on the floor. One, Brother opened, hoping to learn something more. It was from Colonel Steadman to Miriam and me, written a few hours after his death, and contained the sad story of our dear brother's last hours.

He had been in Colonel Steadman's ward of the hospital for more than a week, with headache and sore throat, but it was thought nothing; he seemed to improve, and expected to be discharged in a few days. On the 21st he complained that his throat pained him again. After prescribing for him, and talking cheerfully with him for some time, Colonel Steadman left him surrounded by his friends, to attend to his other patients. He had hardly reached his room when some one ran to him saying Captain Morgan was dying. He hurried to his bedside, and found him dead. Captain Steadman, sick in the next bed, and those around him, said he had been talking pleasantly with them, when he sat up to reach his cup of water on the table. As soon as he drank it he seemed to suffocate; and after tossing his arms wildly in the air, and making several fearful efforts to breathe, he died.

* * *

"Hush, mother, hush," I said when I heard her cries. "We have Brother and George and Jimmy left, and Lydia has lost all!" Heaven pity us! George had gone before—only He in mercy kept the knowledge of it from us for a while longer.

On Thursday the 11th, as we sat talking to mother, striving to make her forget the weary days we had cried through with that fearful sound of "Dead! Dead!" ringing ever in our ears, some one asked for Miriam. She went down, and presently I heard her thanking somebody for a letter. "You could not have brought me anything more acceptable! It is from my sister, though she can hardly have heard from us yet!" I ran back, and sitting at mother's feet, told her Miriam was coming with a letter from Lydia. Mother cried at the mention of her name. O my little sister! You know how dear you are to us! "Mother! Mother!" a horrible voice cried, and before I could think who it was, Miriam rushed in, holding an open letter in her hand, and perfectly wild. "George is dead!" she shrieked, and fell heavily to the ground.

O my God! I could have prayed Thee to take mother, too, when I looked at her. I thought—I almost hoped she was dead, and that pang spared! But I was wild myself. I could have screamed!—laughed! "It is false! Do you hear me, mother? God would not take both! George is not dead!" I cried, trying in vain to arouse her from her horrible state or bring one ray of reason to her eye. I spoke to a body alive only to pain; not a sound of my voice seemed to reach her; only fearful moans showed she was yet alive.

Miriam lay raving on the ground. Poor Miriam! her heart's idol torn away. God help my darling! I did not understand that George *could* die until I looked at her. In vain I strove to raise her from the ground, or check her wild shrieks for death. "George! only George!" she would cry; until at last, with the horror of seeing both die before me, I mastered strength enough to go for the servant and bid her run quickly for Brother.

How long I stood there alone, I never knew. I remember Ada coming in hurriedly and asking what it was. I told her George was dead. It was a relief to see her cry. I could not; but I felt the pain afresh, as though it were her brother she was crying over, not mine. And the sight of her tears brought mine, too. We could only cry over mother and Miriam; we could not rouse them; we did not know what to do.

Some one called me in the entry. I went, not understanding what I was doing. A lady came to me, told me her name, and said something about George; but I could not follow what she said. It was as though she was talking in a dream. I believe she repeated the words several times, for at last she shook me and said, "Listen! Rouse yourself! the letter is about George!" Yes, I said; he is dead. She said I must read the letter; but I could not see, so she read it aloud. It was from Dr. Mitchell, his friend who was with him when he died, telling of his sickness and death. He died on Tuesday the 12th of January, after an illness of six days, conscious to the last and awaiting the end as only a Christian, and one who has led so beautiful a life, could, with the Grace of God, look for it. He sent messages to his brothers and sisters, and bade them tell his mother his last thoughts were of her, and that he died trusting in the mercy of the Saviour. George! our pride! our beautiful, angel brother! *Could* he die? Surely God has sent all these afflictions within these three years to teach us that our hopes must be placed Above, and that it is blasphemy to have earthly idols!

The letter said that the physicians had mistaken his malady, which was inflammation of the bowels, and he had died from being treated for something else. It seemed horrible cruelty to read me that part; I knew that if mother or Miriam ever heard of it, it would kill them. So I begged Mrs. Mitchell never to let them hear of it. She seemed to think nothing of the pain it would inflict; how could she help telling if they asked? she said. I told her I must insist on her not mentioning it; it would only add suffering to what was already insupportable; if they asked for the letter, offer to read it aloud, but say positively that she would not allow any one to touch it except herself, and then she might pass it over in silence. I roused Miriam then and sent her to hear it read. She insisted on reading it herself, and half dead with grief held out her hands, begging piteously to be suffered to read it alone. I watched then until I was sure Mrs. Mitchell would keep her promise. Horrible as I knew it to be from strange lips, I knew by what I experienced that I had saved her from a shock that might cost her her life; and then I went back to mother.

No need to conceal what I felt there! She neither spoke nor saw. If I had shrieked that he died of ill treatment, she would not have understood. But I sat there silently with that horrible secret, wondering if God would help me bear it, or if despair would deprive me of self-control and force me presently to cry it aloud, though it should kill them both.

At last Brother came. I had to meet him downstairs and tell him. God spare me the sight of a strong man's grief! Then Sister came in, knowing as little as he. Poor Sister! I could have blessed her for every tear she shed. It was a comfort to see some one who had life or feeling left. I felt as though the whole world was dead. Nothing was real, nothing existed except horrible speechless pain. Life was a fearful dream through which but one thought ran—"Dead—Dead!"

Miriam had been taken to her room more dead than alive— Mother lay speechless in hers. The shock of this second blow had obliterated, with them, all recollection of the first. It was a mercy I envied them; for I remembered both, until loss of consciousness would have seemed a blessing. I shall never forget mother's shriek of horror when towards evening she recalled it. O those dreadful days of misery and wretchedness! It seems almost sacrilege to refer to them now. They are buried in our hearts with our boys—thought of with prayers and tears.

How will the world seem to us now? What will life be without the boys? When this terrible strife is over, and so many thousands return to their homes, what will peace bring us of all we hoped? Jimmy! Dear Lord, spare us that one!

SOURCE: *A Confederate Girl's Diary*
(Boston, 1913).

SURGEON J. B. MCPHERSON ET AL.

Alexander T. Augusta, a black surgeon who trained in Canada, requested and received appointment to a black Union regiment, the 7th Union South Carolina Infantry. Because his commission was granted several months before those of the white surgeons who signed this letter to President Lincoln, he outranked his white colleagues. Their reaction is indicative of the attitudes of northerners who earnestly supported freedom and just as firmly rejected equality and desegregation. Augusta was transferred to a black recruitment center near Baltimore, but he remained formally attached to the 7th USCI and, upon his promotion to lieutenant colonel, became the highest ranking black officer in the Civil War.

LETTER TO PRESIDENT LINCOLN

Camp Stanton near Bryantown Md. [February 1864]
His
  Excellency,
    Abraham Lincoln
      President U.S.
        Sir,
          We the undersigned, Medical Officers in the Regiments of Colored Troops, under command of Brig. Gen. Wm Birney at this camp, have the honor most respectfully to ask your attention to the following Statement.

When we made applications for positions in the Colored Service, the understanding was universal that *all* Commissioned Officers were to be white men. Judge of our Surprise and disappointment, when upon joining our respective regiments we found that the *Senior Surgeon* of the command was a Negro.

We claim to be behind no one, in a desire for the elevation and improvement of the Colored race, in this Country, and we are willing to sacrifice much, in so grand a cause, as our present positions, may testify. But we cannot in *any* cause, willingly compromise what we consider a proper self respect. Nor do we deem that the interests of either the country or of the Colored race, can demand this of us. Such degradation, we believe to be involved, in our voluntarily continuing in the Service, as Subordinates to a colored officer. We therefore most respectfully, yet earnestly, request, that this *unexpected, unusual,* and most unpleasant relationship in which we have been placed, may in *some way* be terminated.

Most Respectfully Your Obt. Servants,

J. B. McPherson Surgeon 12th Regt U.S.C.I.
E. M. Pease Surg. 9th U.S.C.I.
Chas C Topliff asst Surgeon 19th Regt U.S.C.I
Joel Morse asst Surg 7th U.S.C.I.
M O Carter ass Surgeon 19 Regt
Henry Grange A.S. 7th Regt U.S.C.I.

SOURCE: National Archives, [Feb. 1864], M-118 1864,
Letters Received, ser. 360,
Colored Troops Division, RG 94 [B-11].

JIM HEISKELL

Forced labor of children as well as adults supported the households of slave owners. Nor were children exempt from the cruelties of those owners who were abusive. A year after it was issued, the Emancipation Proclamation made no difference in the life of Jim Heiskell.

AFFIDAVIT OF A TENNESSEE FUGITIVE SLAVE

[Knoxville, Tenn. March 30, 1864]

Statement of "Jim" Heiskell

My name is Jim; I have been living on Bull run, with a man by the name of Pierce; they called him Cromwell Pierce. I run off from him nearly two months ago, because he treated me so mean: he half starved and whipped me. I was whipped three or four times a week, sometimes with a cowhide, and sometimes with a hickory. He put so much work on me, I could not do it; chopping & hauling wood and lumber logs. I am about thirteen years old. I got a pretty good meal at dinner, but he only gave us a half pint of milk for breakfast and supper, with cornbread. I ran away to town; I had a brother "Bob" living in Knoxville, and other boys I knew. I would have staid on the plantation if I had been well used. I wanted also to see some pleasure in town. I hired myself to Capt. Smith as a servant, and went to work as a waiter in Quarter Master Winslow's office as a waiter for the mess. After Capt. Winslow went home, I went to live with Bob, helping him.

Last Friday just after dinner, I saw Pierce Mr. Heiskell's overseer. He caught me on Gay street, he ran after me, and carried me down Cumberland street to Mr. Heiskell's house. Mr. Heiskell, his wife and two sons, and a daughter were in the house. Mr. Heiskell asked me what made me run away; he grabbed me by the back of the ears, and jerked me down on the floor on my face; Mr. Pierce held me & Mr. Heiskell put irons on my legs. Mr. Heiskell took me by the hair of my head, and Mr. Pierce took me around my body, they carried me upstairs, and then Mr. Heiskell dagged me into a room by my hair. They made me stand up, and then they laid me down on my belly & pulled off my breeches as far as they could, and turned my shirt and jacket up over my head. (I heard Mr Heiskell ask for the cowhide before he started with me upstairs.) Mr. Pierce held my legs, and Mr. Heiskell got a straddle of me, and whipped me with the rawhide on my back & legs. Mr. Pierce is a large man, and very strong. Mr. Heiskell rested two or three times, and begun again. I hollowed—"O, Lord" all the time. They whipped me, it seemed to me, half an hour. They then told me to get up and dress, and said if I did'nt behave myself up there they would come up again and whip me again at night. The irons were left on my legs. Mr. Heiskell came up at dark and asked me what that "yellow nigger was talking to me about". He meant my brother Bob, who had been talking to me opposite the house. I was standing up and when he (Mr. Heiskell) asked me about the "yaller nigger", he kicked me with his right foot on my hip and knocked me over on the floor, as the irons were on my feet, I could not catch myself. I knew my brother Bob was around the house trying to get me out. About one hour by sun two soldiers came to the house, one staid & the other went away. I saw them through the window. They had sabres. I thought they had come to guard me to keep Bob from getting me. I heard Bob whisling, and I went to the window and looked through the curtain. Bob told me to hoist the window, put something under it & swing out of the window. I did as my brother told me, and hung by my hands. Bob said "Drop," but I said I was afraid I would hurt myself. Bob said "Wait a minute and I will get a ladder". He brought a ladder and put it against the house, under the window. I got halfway down before they hoisted the window; I fell & Bob caught me and run off with me in his arms. I saw Mr. Pierce sitting at the window, he had a double-barreled gun in his hands. By the time I could count three I heard a gun fired two or three times, quick, I heard Mr. Pierce call "Jim" "Jim" and the guards hollered "halt; halt!" I had no hat or shoes on. We both hid, and laid flat on the ground. I saw the guard, running around there hunting for us. After lying there until the guards had gone away, we got up and Bob carried me to a friend's house. I had the irons on my legs. I got some supper and staid there until next day. My irons were taken off by a colored man, who carried me to the hospital. I am now employed working in the hospital No. 1.

his
—signed—Jim X Heiskell—
mark

SOURCE: *Freedom: A Documentary History of Emancipation 1861–1867*, Sr. 1, Vol. 1, eds. Ira Berlin et al. Cambridge University Press. Reprinted by permission.

GENERAL GEORGE PICKETT

In the spring of 1864 General Pickett, who had suffered such devastating losses in his celebrated charge at Get-tysburg, was endeavoring to ensure the safe evacuation

*of the Confederate capital at Richmond. From the field,
he wrote an almost optimistic letter to his wife.*

LETTER TO HIS WIFE

. . . All is quiet now, but soon all will be bustle, for we march at daylight. Oh, my darling, were there ever such men as those of my division? This morning after the review I thanked them for their valiant services yesterday on the first of April, never to be forgotten by any of us, when, to my mind, they fought one of the most desperate battles of the whole war. Their answer to me was cheer after cheer, one after another calling out, "That's all right, Marse George, we only followed you." . . .

Just after mailing my letter to you at Five Forks, telling you of our long, continuous march of eighteen hours . . . I received a dispatch from the great Tyee telling me to "hold Five Forks at all hazards to prevent the enemy from striking the south side railroad." . . .

I immediately formed line of battle upon the White Oak Road and set my men to throwing up temporary breastworks. Pine trees were felled, a ditch dug and the earth thrown up behind the logs. The men, God bless them, though weary and hungry, sang as they felled and dug. Three times in the three hours their labors were suspended because of attack from the front; but they as cheerily returned to their digging and to their "Annie Laurie" and "Dixie" as if they were banking roses for a festival.

Five Forks is situated in a flat, thickly wooded country and is simply a crossing at right angles of two country roads and a deflection of a third bisecting one of these angles. Our line of battle, short as four small brigades front must be, could readily be turned on either flank by a larger attacking force. Do you understand, my dear? If not, you will some day, and you can keep this letter and show it to someone who will understand.

Well, I made the best arrangements of which the nature of the ground admitted. . . . About two o'clock in the afternoon Sheridan made a heavy demonstration with his cavalry, threatening also the right flank. Meantime Warren's corps swept around the left flank and rear of the infantry line . . . and the attack became general. . . .

I succeeded in getting a sergeant and enough men to man one piece; but after firing eight rounds the axle broke. Floweree's regiment fought hand to hand after all their cartridges had been used. The small cavalry force which had gotten into place gave way, and the enemy poured in. . . . Charge after charge was made and repulsed, and division after division of the enemy advanced upon us. Our left was turned; we were completely entrapped. Their cavalry, charging at a signal of musketry from the infantry, enveloped us front and right and, sweeping down upon our rear, held us as in a vise.

"Take this, Marse George," said one of my boys earlier in the action, hastily thrusting a battle-flag into my hand. I took the flag, stained with his blood, sacred to the cause for which he fell, and, cheering as I waved it, called on my men to get into line to meet the next charge. . . . I rode straight up to where they were and joined in singing, "Rally Once Again," as I waved the blood-stained flag. And, my darling, overpowered, defeated, cut to pieces, starving, captured, as we were, those that were left of us formed front and north and south and met with sullen desperation their double onset. With the members of my own staff and the general officers and their staff officers we compelled a rally . . . enabling many of us to escape capture. . . .

Ah, my Sally, the triumphs of might are transient; but the sufferings and crucifixions for the right can never be forgotten. . . . May God pity those who wait at home for the soldier who has reported to the Great Commander! . . .

The birds were hushed in the woods when I started to write, and now one calls to its mate "Cheer up—cheer up." Let's listen and obey the birds, my darling. . . .

Faithfully your
SOLDIER.

Exeter Mills, April 2, 1865.

SOURCE: The Heart of a Soldier
(New York, 1913).

SPOTSWOOD RICE

This letter from Private Spotswood Rice of Missouri, written while he is recuperating in a hospital, is another reminder of the different views among Americans over the concepts of ownership, freedom, and parental rights.

LETTER TO HIS CHILDREN

From Your Father Spotswood Rice to Mary Ann Corra

My Children I take my pen in hand to rite you A few lines to let you know that I have not forgot you and that I want to see you as bad as ever now my Dear Children I want you to be contented with whatever may be your lots be assured that I will have you if it cost me my life on the 28th of the mounth. 8 hundred White and 8 hundred blacke solders expects to start up the rivore to Glasgow and above there that thats to be jeneraled by a jeneral that will give me both of you when they Come I expect to be with them and expect to get you both in return. Dont be uneasy my children I expect to have you. If Diggs dont give you up this Government will and I feel confident that I will get you Your Miss Kaitty Said that I tried to steal you But I'll let her know that god never intended for man to steal his own flesh and blood. If I had no cofidence in God I could have confidence in her But as it is If I ever had any Confidence in her I have none now and never expect to have And I want her to remember if She meets me with ten thousand soldiers She [will?] meet her enemy. I once thout I had Some respect for them but now my respects is worn out and have no sympathy for Slaveholders. And as for her cristianantty I expect the Devil has Such in hell You tell her from me that She is the frist Christian that I ever heard say that aman could Steal his own child especially out of human bondage

You can tell her that She can hold to you as long as she can I never would expect to ask her again to let you come to me because I know that the devil has got her hot set againts that that is write now my Dear children I am a going to close my letter to you Give my love to all enquiring friends tell them all that we are well and want to see them very much and Corra and Mary receive the greater part of it you sefves and dont think hard of us not sending you any thing I you father have a plenty for you when I see you Spott & Noah sends their love to both of you Oh! My Dear children how I do want to see you

SOURCE: National Archives, [3 Sept. 1864], enclosed in F.W. Diggs to Genl. Rosecrans, 10 Sept. 1864, D-296 1864, Letters Received, ser. 2593, Dept. of the MO, RG 393 Pt. 1 [C-154].

CHARLES MINOR BLACKFORD

For almost half of her life, Nannie, Charles Blackford's oldest daughter, must have been familiar with her father's letters describing camp life and events of the war. While this letter is not the typical one a father might write to his seven-year-old daughter, it vividly describes the scene before him.

LETTER TO NANNIE

We are camped in a very sweet grove by the side of a large brick house, and I often wish you and your mother were here to enjoy it. I would like for you to see Drury's Bluff and the big cannon down there—bigger than any two in Colonel Huger's battalion—big enough for you almost to crawl into. The breastworks there are very high, and they have little rooms in them in which the powder and shells and shot are kept so they may not be injured either by rain or the shells of the enemy. The fortifications are all turfed, which makes them look much nicer than any you have ever seen. The soldiers live in small cabins, all of which are white-washed, and they have beautiful walkways between them and flowers and grass to make them look better. Would you not like such soldiering as that? This fort is so situated that we can sink the yankee gunboats with our big guns if they try to pass up the James river, which is just at the foot of the bluff, to Richmond. . . . We are camped on a place where there was a battle fought three months ago, and there are many curious signs of it now left. Very near us the yankees had their field hospital, and many of them are buried all around us. In one hole they threw all the legs and arms they cut off, and as they only threw a little dirt over them many of them are sticking out now, making a very horrid sight, but one we get used to. All the trees around us are marked by cannon and musket balls, as the battle raged all around the house, in the yard, and in the porch room. A shell from one of our batteries struck a large oak tree and went to the heart of it before it exploded; then one piece of the shell went up the heart of the tree and the other down. It split the tree, of course, but stuck fast and stands there now like a great wedge, a monument to the power of cannon and to the fierceness of war. I hope the owner of the place will let it stand as it is, as a memento of the times, which will be very striking when you are an old woman. Another large tree has a great shell sticking in it, but it did not burst.

The most remarkable thing I have seen is in a cabin, a few hundred yards from here, where a dead yankee is lying still unburied. He seems to have been wounded and carried to this cabin and laid on some straw on its floor. There he died, and had, as many bodies do, just dried up, for the cabin was between the two lines, and neither side could get to him to aid him or bury him. Right by his side lies the body of a great Newfoundland dog, which the negroes at the house, in the yard of which we are camped, say died of starvation rather than leave his dead master. Master and dog lie there together, strangers in the land of their enemies, unburied and unwept, and, perhaps, far away in the North, he has some little girl like you who is still hoping for her father's return, and picturing the joy of having him back and of romping with the faithful dog. War is a sad thing, but if the poor man had staid at home and not come down here to desolate our homes and murder you and your mother and burn our houses, he would have been with his little girl now, and she could have played with her dog as long as he lived. The negroes told us that they tried to get him to leave his master, and tempted him with food. Once he came out and eat something, but went back and afterwards they could not get him to leave his place or to eat anything. So, there he died. Men are not so faithful as dogs.

SOURCE: *Memoirs of Life In and Out of the Army in Virginia During the War Between the States* (Lynchburg, Va., 1894–96).

ELLA GERTRUDE CLANTON THOMAS

Toward the end of the war, some southerners began privately to question the institution of slavery. Like Ella Gertrude Clanton Thomas, they desired an end to the war and its restrictions on their lives; at the same time, they remained steadfast in their desire for southern autonomy.

from THE SECRET EYE

Saturday, September 17, 1864 . . . How I do wish this war was over. I wish to breathe free. I feel pent up, confined—cramped and shall I confess it am reminded of that Italian story of *The Iron Shroud* where daily—daily hourly and momently the room contracts, the victim meanwhile utterly impotent to avert the impending doom. Never have I so fully realised the feeble hold upon this world's goods as I do now. I don't think I have ever enjoyed that peculiarly charming season the Indian Summer more than I have during the past few weeks. Looking up the three Avenues and at the Goats Cows and Horses so quietly walking about, listening at the cooing of Pigions, the chirping of the different fowls in the yard—I imagine this contrasted with men clad in Yankee uniform rudely violating the privacy of my home. I imagine the booming of Yankee cannon and the clash of Yankee sabres and I ask myself how soon shall this thing be?? Nor does it require an imaginative mind to foretell such an event but the last page of my Journal must bear no such cowardly record.

I have sometimes doubted on the subject of slavery. I have seen so many of its evils chief among which is the terribly demoralising influence upon our men and boys but of late I have become convinced the Negro *as a race* is better off with us as he has been than if he were made free, but I am by no means so sure that we would not gain by his having his freedom given him. I grant that I am not so philanthropic as to be willing voluntarily to give all we own for the sake of the principle, but I do think that if we had the same invested in something else as a means of support I would willingly, nay gladly, have the responsibility of them taken off my shoulders.

This Journal was commenced July 13th 1861 and I am ashamed that three years of the most eventful period of my life should have had so poor a record but I find that the absorbing theme of war is one to be talked of better than written about and what I write is so commonplace when contrasted with the stirring events to which I allude that I shrink from making a record of them. I have cut out for the scrap books (which I cannot buy) an account of all the important events which have taken place. . . . Again political events have absorbed so much of my Journal to the exclusion of domestic matters that one might readily suppose that I was not the happy mother of four darling children. . . .

SOURCE: *The Secret Eye: The Journal of Ella Gertrude Clanton Thomas, 1848–1889*, edited by Virginia Ingraham Burr. Copyright © 1990 by Virginia Ingraham Burr and Gertrude T. Despeaux. Reprinted by permission of the publisher.

DOLLY SUMNER LUNT BURGE

On his campaign through Georgia, General Sherman ordered his troops to forage for supplies. His recommendations to bypass poor families and to leave minimum provisions for a family were frequently ignored, and foraging often escalated into outright looting. Dolly Sumner Lunt Burge describes the pillaging of her homestead.

SHERMAN'S ARMY

[Nov.] 19th. . . I walked to the gate. There they came, filing up. I hastened back to my frightened servants & told them they had better hide, & then went back to the gate to claim protection & a guard. But like Demons they rush in. My yards are full. To my smokehouse, my dairy, pantry, kitchen & cellar like famished wolves they come, breaking locks & whatever is in their way. The thousand pounds of meat in my smokehouse is gone in a twinkling. My flour, my meat, my lard, butter, eggs, pickles of various kinds, both in vinegar & brine, wine, jars & jugs, are all gone. My eighteen fat turkeys my hens, chickens & fowls—my young pigs, are shot down in my yard, & hunted as if they were the rebels themselves. Utterly powerless, I came to appeal to the guard I cannot help you Madam it is the orders & as I stood there from my lot, I saw driven first old Dutch my dear old Buggy horse, who had carried my dear dead husband so many miles, & who would so quietly wait at the block for him to mount & dismount, & then had carried him to his grave, performing the same sad office to dear Lou—& who had been my faithful servant so many years. Then old Mary, my brood mare, who for years has been too old & stiff, for work. With her three year old colt my two year old mule, & her last little baby colt—there they go—There go my sheep & worse than all—my boys, my poor boys, are forced to get the mules.

But alas little did I think while trying to save my house from plunder & fire—that they were forcing at the point of the bayonet my boys from home. One . . . jumped into the bed in his cabin, & declared himself sick, another crawled under the floor, a lame boy, he was, but they pulled him out & placed him on a horse & drove him off. Kid, poor kid. The last I saw of him, a man had him going round the garden looking as I thought for my sheep as he was my shepherd. Jack came crying to me the big tears coursing down his cheeks saying they were making him go. I said stay in my room but a man followed in cursing him & threatening to shoot him if he did not go poor Jack had to yield. James Arnold in trying to escape from a back window was captured & marched off. Henry too was taken I know not how or when, but probably when he & Bob went after the mules.

I had not believed they would force from their homes the poor doomed negroes, but such has been the fact here, cursing them & saying that Jeff Davis was going to put them in his army, but they should not fight for him but for them. No indeed! No! They are not friends to the slave We have never made the poor cowardly negro fight, & it is strange, passing strange, that the all powerful Yankee nation with the whole world to back them, their ports open, their armies filled with soldiers from all nations, should at last take the poor negro to help them out against this "little Confederacy," which was to be brought back into the Union in sixty days time. My poor boys, My poor boys. What unknown trials are before you. How Jon here clung to your mistress & assisted her in every way you knew how you have never known want, of any kind, never have I corrected them a word was sufficient it was only to tell them what I wanted done & they obeyed. Their parents are with me & how sadly they lament the loss of their boys.

Their cabins are rifled of every valuable. The soldiers swearing that their Sunday clothes were the white peoples & that they never had time to get such things as they had. Poor . . . chest was broken open, his money & tobacco taken, he has always been a money making & saving boy, not unfrequently has his crop brought him five hundred dollars & more. All of his clothes and Rachels clothes that dear Lou gave her before her death & which she had packed away were stolen from her. Ovens, skillets, coffee mills of which we had three, coffee pots, not one have I left—sifters all gone. Seeing that the soldiers could not be restrained the guard ordered me to have their things that remained brought into my house. Which I did—& they all, poor things, huddled together into my room fearing every moment that the house would be burned.

A Mr. Webber from Illinois & a Captain came into my house of whom I claimed protection from the vandals that were forcing themselves into my rooms. He said he knew my brother Orrington of Chicago, at that name I could not restrain my feelings but bursting into tears implored him to see my brother & let him know my destitution. I saw nothing before me but starvation. He promised to do this & comforted me with the assurance that my dwelling house would not be burned though my out buildings might. Poor little Sadie went crying to him as a friend & told him they had her doll Nancy he begged her to come & see him & he would give her a fine waxen one. He felt for me & I give him & several others the character of gentlemen. I don't believe they would have molested women & children had they had their own way. He seemed surprised that I had not laid away in my house flour & other provisions. I did not suppose I could secure them there more than where I usually kept them for in last summer raid houses were thoroughly searched. In parting with him I parted as with a friend.

Sherman with a greater portion of his army passed my house all day. All day, as its sad moments rolled on were they passing, not only in front of my house, but they came up behind, tore down my garden palings, made a road through my back yard & lot field, driving their stock & riding through, tearing down my fences, & desolating my home Wantonly doing it when there was no necessity for it. Such a day if I live to the age of Methuselah, may God spare me from ever seeing again.

Such were some of the scenes of this sad day and as night drew its sable curtains around us, the heavens from every point were lit up with flames from burning buildings! Dinnerless & supperless as we were, it was nothing in comparison to the fear of being driven out homeless & houseless to the dreary woods. Nothing to eat. I could give my guard no supper & he left us. I appealed to another asking him if he had wife mother or sister, & how he should feel were they in my situation. A Col. from Vermont left me two men but they were Dutch & I could not understand one word they said. My Heavenly Father alone saved me from the destructive fire. Carriage house had in it eight bales of cotton with my carriage buggy & harness, on top of the cotton was some corded cotton rolls a hundred pounds or more. These were thrown out the blankets in which they were taken, & a large twist of the rolls, set on fire & thrown into the boat of my carriage which was close up to the cotton bales. Thanks to my God the cotton only burned over & then went out! Shall I ever forget the deliverance?

This was after night—the greater part of the army had passed. It came up very windy and cold. My room was full nearly with the bedding of 8 with the negroes. They were afraid to go out for my women could not step outside of the door without an insult from them. They lay down on the floor Sadie got down & under the same cover with Sally while I sat up all night. Watching every moment for the flames to burst out from some of my buildings. The two guards came into my room & laid themselves by my fire. For the night I could not close my eyes but kept walking to & fro. Watching the fires in the distance & dreading the approaching day which I feared as they had not all passed would be but a continuation of horrors.

SOURCE: American Women's Diaries, 1789–1923.
Microfilm. Manuscripts and Archives,
Yale University.

JEFFERSON DAVIS

As the cause was being lost on the battlefield in the autumn of 1864, Confederate President Jefferson Davis delivered an exhausting round of speeches to bolster the spirits of those at home. Southerners greeted him with great applause even as their fortunes, economic and military, were sinking all across the region.

SPEECH, COLUMBIA, SOUTH CAROLINA

Thursday, Oct 6, 1864.

Ladies and Gentlemen of the Metropolis of South Carolina—
. . . South Carolina has struggled nobly in the war and suffered many sacrifices. There is, indeed, no portion of our land where the pall of mourning has not been spread; but I thank the Giver of all Good that our people still remain firm there, above all other places. I am told there have been none to waver and none to doubt. It often happens that at a distance from a scene of action, men, who if present would easily measure it, magnify danger, until at last those become despondent whose hearts, if actually stirred by perils, would no sooner think of shrinking from the prompt performance of duty, than the gallant

sons of Carolina, whose blood has so generously flowed on the many battle fields of this war. But if there be any who feel that our cause is in danger; that final success may not crown our efforts; that we are not stronger to-day than when we began this struggle; that we are not able to continue the supplies to our armies and to our people, let all such read a contradiction in the smiling face of our land, and the teeming evidences of plenty which everywhere greet the eye; let them go to those places where brave men are standing in front of the foe, and there receive the assurance that we shall have final success, and that every man who does not live to see his country free, will see a freeman's grave.

There are those who, like the Israelites of old, are longing to turn back to the fleshpots they have left; who have thought there may still be some feasible mode of reconciliation and would even be willing to rush into a reconstruction of the Union. Such, I am glad to know, do not flourish on the soil of South Carolina. Such cannot be the sentiment of any man in the Confederate States, if he will only recollect that from the beginning down to the present hour, your Government has made every effort within its power, to avoid a collision of arms in the first instance; and since then to obtain every possible means of settlement honorable to ourselves, based on a recognition of our independence. First, we sent commissioners to ask on what terms the quarrel could be adjusted, and since that time we have proclaimed in every public place our desire for peace. Insolently our every effort has been met. The Vice-President of the Confederate States was refused a passport to the North, when his object was negotiation—that means by which all wars must be terminated. The door was rudely shut in our faces. Intervention and recognition by foreign States, so long anticipated, has proved an *ignus fatuus*. There is, then, but one means by which you can hope to gain independence and an honorable peace, and that is by uniting with harmony, energy and determination in fighting those great battles and achieving those great victories, which will teach the world that we can defend our rights, and the Yankee nation that it is death to invade them.

With every Confederate victory our stocks rise in the foreign market—that touchstone of European sentiment. With every noble achievement that influences the public mind abroad, you are taking one step forward, and bringing foreign nations one step nearer your aid in recognizing and lending you friendly intervention, whenever they are satisfied that, intervention or no intervention, the Confederacy can sustain itself.

Does any one believe that Yankees are to be conciliated by terms of concession? Does any man imagine that we can conquer the Yankees by retreating before them, or do you not all know that the only way to make spaniels civil is to whip them? And you can whip them, if all the men capable of bearing arms will do their duty by taking their places under the standard of their country, before the veteran troops of the North receive the fresh increment which is being gathered in the Northern States. Now is the good and accepted time for every man to rally to the standard of his country and crush the invader upon her soil; and this, I believe, is in your power. If every man fit to bear arms will place himself in the ranks with those who are already there, we shall not battle in vain, and our achievement will be grand, final and complete. Is this a time to ask what the law demands of you—to inquire whether or not you are exempt under the law, or to ask if the magistrate will take you out of the enrolling office by a writ of *habeas corpus*? Rather is it not the time for every man capable of bearing arms to say: "My country needs my services, and my country shall have them!" When your heroic fathers, the Whigs of the Revolution, fought in that war which secured your birthright, their armies were not gathered by asking who can be forced into the field? but "who are able to fight?" No man was too old and no boy too young, if he had the physical capacity to enter the ranks of the army. In the days of the Revolution, the boy left his paternal roof only to return to its blackened ruins. He grew to manhood among its struggles; and may not your country claim similar services from the youth of the present day? Like them, you must emulate the glory of your sires. Say not that you are unequal to the task, for I believe that our people are even better than were our honored ancestors. They have fought more and bloodier battles, and there are fewer who are luke-warm in the cause now, than existed in the days of the Revolution. What a glorious reflection it is, that wherever the tide of war has rolled its devastating wave over the land, just then do you find every heart beating true to the Confederacy, strengthened, as it were, by vicissitudes, and every woman ready to share her last loaf with the soldier who is fighting for our rights. . . .

It is scarcely necessary for me, at a time like this, to argue grave questions, respecting policy, past, present or prospective. I only ask you to have faith and confidence, and to believe that every faculty of my head and my heart is devoted to your cause, and to that I shall, if necessary, give my life. Let every one in his own sphere and according to his own capacity, devote himself to the single purpose of filling up and sustaining our armies in the field. If required to stay at home, let him devote himself not to the acquisition of wealth, but to the advancement of the common cause. If there is to be any aristocracy in the land after this war, I hope that it will be an aristocracy of those men who have become poor while bleeding to secure liberty. If there are to be any peculiarly favored by public opinion hereafter, I trust it will be those men who have longest borne a musket and oftenest bled upon the battle fields. If there is to be any man shunned by the young ladies when he seeks their favor, I trust it will be the man who has grown rich by skulking.

And with all sincerity, I say to my young friends here, if you want the right man for a husband, take him whose armless sleeve and noble heart betoken the duties that he has rendered to his country, rather than he who has never shared the toils, or borne the dangers of the field. If there still be left any of those military critics who have never spoken of our generals but to show how much better things could have been managed, or of our Government, but to find fault with it, because it never took their advice—in mercy's name let these wise men go to the front and aid us in achieving our independence. With their wisdom and strength swelling our armies, I should have some hopes that I will not be a corpse before our cause is secured, and that our flag would never trail in dishonor, but would wave victoriously above the roar and smoke of battle. . . .

SOURCE: *Jefferson Davis, Constitutionalist: His Letters, Papers and Speeches*, edited by Dunbar Rowland (Jackson, Miss., 1923).

COLORED MEN OF THE UNITED STATES
The idea of slavery and discrimination as the violation of the natural rights of human beings had gained only the most partial acceptance in the North at the start of the war and was by no means unanimous at the end of the armed conflict. It remained necessary for northern black voices to articulate the important rights a democratic republic still denied them.

DECLARATION OF WRONGS AND RIGHTS,
Made by the Colored Men of the United States of America in Convention Assembled, in Syracuse, N.Y., Oct. 4, 1864.

1st. As a branch of the human family, we have for long ages been deeply and cruelly wronged by people whose might constituted their right; we have been subdued, not by the power of ideas, but by brute force, and have been unjustly deprived not only of many of our natural rights, but debarred the privileges and advantages freely accorded to other men.

2d. We have been made to suffer well-nigh every cruelty and indignity possible to be heaped upon human beings; and for no fault of our own.

3d. We have been taunted with our inferiority by people whose statute-books contained laws inflicting the severest penalties on whomsoever dared teach us the art of reading God's word; we have been denounced as incurably ignorant, and, at the same time, have been, by stern enactments, debarred from taking even the first step toward self-enlightenment and personal and national elevation; we have been declared incapable of self-government by those who refused us the right of experiment in that direction, and we have been denounced as cowards by men who refused at first to trust us with a musket on the battle-field.

4th. As a people, we have been denied the ownership of our bodies, our wives, homes, children, and the products of our own labor; we have been compelled, under pain of death, to submit to wrongs deeper and darker than the earth ever witnessed in the case of any other people; we have been forced to silence and inaction in full presence of the infernal spectacle of our sons groaning under the lash, our daughters ravished, our wives violated, and our firesides desolated, while we ourselves have been led to the shambles and sold like beasts of the field.

5th. When the nation in her trial hour called her sable sons to arms, we gladly went to fight her battles: but were denied the pay accorded to others, until public opinion demanded it; and then it was tardily granted. We have fought and conquered, but have been denied the laurels of victory. We have fought where victory gave us no glory, and where captivity meant cool murder on the field, by fire, sword, and halter; and yet no black man ever flinched.

6th. We are taxed, but denied the right of representation. We are practically debarred the right of trial by jury; and institutions of learning which we help to support are closed against us.

We submit to the American people and world the following Declaration of our Rights, asking a calm consideration thereof:

1st. We declare that all men are born free and equal; that no man or government has a right to annul, repeal, abrogate, contravene, or render inoperative, this fundamental principle, except it be for crime; therefore we demand the immediate and unconditional abolition of slavery.

2d. That, as natives of American soil, we claim the right to remain upon it: and that any attempt to deport, remove, expatriate, or colonize us to any other land, or to mass us here against our will, is unjust; for here were we born, for this country our fathers and our brothers have fought, and here we hope to remain in the full enjoyment of enfranchised manhood, and its dignities.

3d. That, as citizens of the Republic, we claim the rights of other citizens. We claim that we are, by right, entitled to respect; that due attention should be given to our needs; that proper rewards should be given for our services, and that the immunities and privileges of all other citizens and defenders of the nation's honor should be conceded to us. We claim the right to be heard in the halls of Congress; and we claim our fair share of the public domain, whether acquired by purchase, treaty, confiscation, or military conquest.

4th. That, emerging as we are from the long night of gloom and sorrow, we are entitled to, and claim, the sympathy and aid of the entire Christian world; and we invoke the considerate aid of mankind in this crisis of our history, and in this hour of sacrifice, suffering, and trial.

Those are our wrongs; these a portion of what we deem to be our rights as men, as patriots, as citizens, and as children of the common Father. To realize and attain these rights, and their practical recognition, is our purpose. We confide our cause to the just God, whose benign aid we solemnly invoke. To him we appeal.

SOURCE: *Proceedings of the National Convention of Colored Men, held in the City of Syracuse, N.Y., Oct. 4, 5, 6, and 7, 1864; with the Bill of Wrongs and Rights, and the Address to the American People* (Boston, 1864). Reprinted with permission from the Schomburg Center for Research in Black Culture, New York Public Library. Astor, Lenox and Tilden Foundations.

ANONYMOUS

By the end of 1864, the situation was desperate not only for the southern military but also for their cold and hungry families. One Confederate soldier named Billy received this letter from his wife. He deserted the army to attend to his family only to be court-martialed upon his return to the field. Before his execution, however, the Confederate government in Richmond reprieved all deserters.

LETTER, DEC. 17, 1864

B — N —, Dec. 17, 1864.

My Dear B—: Christmus is most hear again, and things is worse and worse. I have got my last kalica frock on, and that's patched. Everything me and children's got is patched. Both of them is in bed now covered up with comforters and old pieces of karpet to keep them warm, while I went 'long out to try and get some wood, for their feet's on the ground and they have got no clothes, neither; and I am not able to cut the wood, and me and the children have broke up all the rails 'roun' the yard and picked up all the chips there is. We haven't got nothing in the house to eat but a little bit o' meal. The last pound of meet you got from Mr. G— is all eat up, and so is the chickens we raised. I don't want you to stop fighten them yankees till you kill the last one of them, but try and get off and come home and fix us all up some and then you can go back and fight them a heep harder than you ever fought them before. We can't none of us hold out much longer down hear. One of General Mahone's skouts promis me on his word to carry this letter through the lines to you, but, my dear, if you put off a-comin' 'twon't be no use to come, for we'll all hands of us be out there in the garden in the old graveyard with your ma and mine.

SOURCE: *Pickett and His Men*
by LaSalle Corbell Pickett
(Atlanta, 1899).

WALT WHITMAN

For most of the war, Walt Whitman lived in Washington, D.C., and worked as a government clerk and as a writer for northern newspapers. He continued writing poetry while nursing sick and wounded Union and Confederate soldiers in Washington hospitals.

THE WOUND-DRESSER

1

An old man bending I come among new faces,
Years looking backward resuming in answer to children,
Come tell us old man, as from young men and maidens that love me,
(Arous'd and angry, I'd thought to beat the alarum, and urge
    relentless war,
But soon my fingers fail'd me, my face droop'd and I resign'd myself,
To sit by the wounded and soothe them, or silently watch the dead;)
Years hence of these scenes, of these furious passions, these
    chances,
Of unsurpassed heroes, (was one side so brave? the other was
    equally brave;)
Now be witness again, paint the mightiest armies of earth,
Of those armies so rapid so wondrous what saw you to tell us?

What stays with you latest and deepest? of curious panics,
Of hard-fought engagements or sieges tremendous what deepest
    remains?

2

O maidens and young men I love and that love me,
What you ask of my days those the strangest and sudden your
    talking recalls,
Soldier alert I arrive after a long march cover'd with sweat and dust,
In the nick of time I come, plunge in the fight, loudly shout in
    the rush of successful charge,
Enter the captur'd works—yet lo, like a swift-running river they fade,
Pass and are gone they fade—I dwell not on soldiers' perils or
    soldiers' joys,
(Both I remember well—many the hardships, few the joys, yet I
    was content.)

But in silence, in dreams' projections,
While the world of gain and appearance and mirth goes on,
So soon what is over forgotten, and waves wash the imprints off
    the sand,
With hinged knees returning I enter the doors, (while for you up there,
Whoever you are, follow without noise and be of strong heart.)

Bearing the bandages, water and sponge,
Straight and swift to my wounded I go,
Where they lie on the ground after the battle brought in,
Where their priceless blood reddens the grass the ground,
Or to the rows of the hospital tent, or under the roof'd hospital,
To the long rows of cots up and down each side I return,
To each and all one after another I draw near, not one do I miss,
An attendant follows holding a tray, he carries a refuse pail,
Soon to be fill'd with clotted rags and blood, emptied, and fill'd again.

I onward go, I stop,
With hinged knees and steady hand to dress wounds,
I am firm with each, the pangs are sharp yet unavoidable,
One turns to me his appealing eyes—poor boy! I never knew you,
Yet I think I could not refuse this moment to die for you, if that
    would save you.

3

On, on I go, (open doors of time! open hospital doors!)
The crush'd head I dress, (poor crazed hand tear not the bandage
    away,)

The neck of the cavalry-man with the bullet through and through
    I examine,
Hard the breathing rattles, quite glazed already the eye, yet life
    struggles hard,
(Come, sweet death! be persuaded O beautiful death!
    In mercy come quickly.)

From the stump of the arm, the amputated hand,
I undo the clotted lint, remove the slough, wash off the matter
    and blood,
Back on his pillow the soldier bends with curv'd neck and side-
    falling head,
His eyes are closed, his face is pale, he dares not look on the
    bloody stump,
And has not yet look'd on it.

I dress a wound in the side, deep, deep,
But a day or two more, for see the frame all wasted and sinking,
And the yellow-blue countenance see.

I dress the perforated shoulder, the foot with the bullet wound,
Cleanse the one with a gnawing and putrid gangrene, so sicken-
    ing, so offensive,
While the attendant stands behind aside me holding the tray and pail.

I am faithful, I do not give out,
The fractur'd thigh, the knee, the wound in the abdomen,
These and more I dress with impassive hand, (yet deep in my
    breast a fire, a burning flame.)

4

Thus in silence in dreams' projections,
Returning, resuming, I thread my way through the hospitals,
The hurt and wounded I pacify with soothing hand,
I sit by the restless all the dark night, some are so young,
Some suffer so much, I recall the experience sweet and sad,
(Many a soldier's loving arms about this neck have cross'd and
    rested,
Many a soldier's kiss dwells on these bearded lips.)

RECONCILIATION

Word over all, beautiful as the sky,
Beautiful that war and all its deeds of carnage must in time be
    utterly lost,

That the hands of the sisters Death and Night incessantly softly
    wash again, and ever again, this soil'd world;
For my enemy is dead, a man divine as myself is dead,
I look where he lies white-faced and still in the coffin—I draw near,
Bend down and touch lightly with my lips the white face in the
    coffin.

SOURCE: *Leaves of Grass*
(Philadelphia, 1883).

GIDEON

*While the military fortunes of the Confederacy shift over
the course of the war, the public ideological arguments
do not. In this front page article in South Carolina's
Charleston Daily Courier, on January 24, 1865, an anonymous writer uses the pseudonym of Gideon, an Old
Testament Israelite warrior who was victorious against
oppression. The terms and rhetoric, Biblical and political,
echo those employed by Rev. Benjamin Palmer in his
New Orleans speech four years earlier.*

SLAVERY AND STATE SOVEREIGNTY

It is to maintain slavery, God's institution of labor, and the primary
political element of our Confederate form of Government, state sovereignty, that we have taken the sword of justice against the infidel and
oppressor. The two must stand or fall together. To talk of maintaining
our independence while we abolish slavery is simply to talk folly. Four
millions of our fellow men, in the domestic relation of slaves have, in
the providence of God, under His unalterable decree have been committed to our charge. We dare not abandon them to the tender mercies
of the infidel. . . .

African slave labor is the only form of labor whereby our soil can
be cultivated, and the great staples of our clime produced. The testimony of ample experience proves that the white man is not physically
adapted to that end, and he sickens, degenerates and dies, if he un-
dertakes it. By the removal of African slave labor from this land, our
productive and fruitful fields must become barren waste and impene-
trable swamps. By yielding to Abolition infidelity, and emancipating
our slaves, we will destroy the household, disorganize the family, and
annihilate our Government—act contrary to the will and instruction of
God—bring down His just wrath upon our heads, and doom ourselves
to utter humiliation, contempt and wretchedness as a people. The last

hope of true Republican liberty on the American continent would
be lost, the progresss of the human family, by the light of religion, science and true philosophy, toward peace and happiness, blackened for
centuries, and the triumph of the rulers of darkness of this world advanced. Man's allegience to God is liberty. What power soever inter-
venes between man and his Maker, and interferes with that obedience
revealed in the Word of God, as due to Him alone, is unlawful, tyran-
nical, despotic, it is the power of the devil and his followers, to be re-
sisted unto blood and vanquished with a sword. . . .

Without a revelation from the Creator to his creature, man could
no more have understood the history and object of his being than can
the untutored savage, by intuition, acquire a correct knowledge of the
history of the world and of the discoveries and achievements of science. Unaided reason could not conduct him by the moral sense, nor
could Nature, the handmaid of God, lead him, by the affections, back
to his God and to happiness; another light was needed to guide, another Mediator to restore him.

The woman was beguiled by the devil from her allegience to her
Maker, she gave of the tree to ADAM, and she did eat. The conflict between the seed of the woman (not wholly corrupted or lost, or God
would have abandoned them) and the seed of the devil was begun; the
race of Adam was doomed to labor, mental and physical. The corrupted nature of man developed selfishness, and the inevitable struggle between might and right was commenced; the strong, physically or
morally, would oppress the weak, and appropriate the fruits of his
labor. The divine decree dooming him to labor was unalterably attached to the existence of man; God, known unto whom are all his
ways, determined to legitimize it, and to introduce it, perfected by His
Gospel, into His system of government of the human race. He inflicted
it as a punishment on Canaan, incorporated into His law, and provided for its being perfected by the teachings of His Gospel, and converted into a blessing instead of a curse.

This is the history of slavery, the intention of God, what the Abolition fanatics would overthrow, what God has entrusted to this Christian people, this Confederation of states, to maintain. It is incorporated
into their very being as a people, their existence as a Confederation,
their independence as sovereign states. Without slavery, God's institution of slavery, a Constitutional Republican form of government, the
form most in accord with the spirit and genius of Christianity, and
which has been bought and established for us by the blood and wisdom of our patriot sires and sages, cannot exist. A Republic without
slavery is an impossibility. Under a Republican form of government
each citizen has a right to elevate himself to the highest positions, to
become one of the rulers, or by the ballot to place those of his choice

in the position of rulers; and he who is occupied in servile duties can never acquire or possess the necessary knowledge and learning to exercise this right.

The overthrow of the former United States is an existing demonstration of this political truth. The servant cannot, in the nature of things, possess the right to elevate himself above his lord. Had slavery existed not only by the constitution of the former United States, but actually in all the States composing that Confederation, it would have stood to the end of time and government. The last hope of true liberty and Republican Government rests with us. The maintenance of that system of labor which Divine Wisdom has established is committed to our charge. Abandon our inheritance—Liberty—and prove faithless to the charge committed to us by God. His wrath and the curses of millions yet unborn will rest upon us. . . .

SOURCE: *Charleston Daily Courier,*
January 24, 1865.

LUTHER RICE MILLS

In March of 1865, Luther Rice Mills had been in the Confederate army for four years and was now under General Lee defending Petersburg, Virginia. This city had been under Union siege for almost nine months, the lengthiest offensive of the war. Numerous times, Lee tried to break through the Union lines but they held. In this letter to his brother, Mills communicates the physical and psychological conditions of the Confederate forces just before the end of the war.

LETTER TO JOHN MILLS

March 2nd, 1865

BROTHER JOHN:

Something is about to happen. I know not what. Nearly every one who will express an opinion says Gen'l Lee is about to evacuate Petersburg. The authorities are having all the cotton, tobacco &c. moved out of the place as rapidly as possible. This was commenced about the 22nd of February. Two thirds of the Artillery of our Division has been moved out. The Reserved Ordnance Train has been loaded up and is ready to move at any time. I think Gen'l Lee expects a hard fight on the right and has ordered all this simply as a precautionary measure. Since my visit to the right I have changed my opinion about the necessity for the evacuation of Petersburg. If it is evacuated Johnson's Division will be in a bad situation for getting out. Unless we are so fortunate as to give the Yankees the slip many of us will be captured. I would regret very much to have to give up the old place. The soiled and tattered Colors borne by our skeleton Regiments is sacred and dear to the hearts of every man. No one would exchange it for a new flag. So it is with us. I go down the lines, I see the marks of shot and shell, I see where fell my comrades, the Crater, the grave of fifteen hundred Yankees, when I go to the rear I see little mounds of dirt some with headboards, some with none, some with shoes protruding, some with a small pile of bones on one side near the end showing where a hand was left uncovered, in fact everything near shows desperate fighting. And here I would rather "fight it out." If Petersburg and Richmond is evacuated—from what I have seen & heard in the army—our cause will be hopeless. It is useless to conceal the truth any longer. Many of our people at home have become so demoralized that they write to their husbands, sons and brothers that desertion *now* is not *dishonorable.* It would be impossible to keep the army from straggling to a ruinous extent if we evacuate. I have just received an order from Wise to carry out on picket tonight a rifle and ten rounds of Cartridges to shoot men when they desert. The men seem to think desertion no crime & hence never shoot a deserter when he goes over—they always shoot but never hit. I am glad to say that we have not had but four desertions from our Reg't to the enemy. . . .

Write soon.

Yours Truly

L. R. MILLS

Source: *Letters of Luther Rice Mills: A Confederate Soldier,*
edited by George D. Harmon (Raleigh, N.C., 1927).
Reprinted with permission of the
North Carolina Historical Review.

ABRAHAM LINCOLN

Running as a candidate for the Union Party, a combination of Republican and Democratic supporters of the war, Lincoln defeated Gen. McClellan, former commander of the Union army and Democratic presidential candidate in 1864. In full recognition that the war is over slavery and that conscience demands that institution's defeat,

Lincoln's second inaugural address transcends his previous pronouncements.

SECOND INAUGURAL ADDRESS

March 4, 1865

FELLOW COUNTRYMEN:—At this second appearing to take the oath of the Presidential office, there is less occasion for an extended address than there was at the first. Then a statement somewhat in detail of a course to be pursued seemed very fitting and proper. Now, at the expiration of four years, during which public declarations have been constantly called forth on every point and phase of the great contest which still absorbs the attention and engrosses the energies of the nation, little that is new could be presented.

The progress of our arms, upon which all else chiefly depends, is as well known to the public as to myself, and it is, I trust, reasonably satisfactory and encouraging to all. With high hope for the future, no prediction in regard to it is ventured.

On the occasion corresponding to this four years ago, all thoughts were anxiously directed to an impending civil war. All dreaded it, all sought to avoid it. While the inaugural address was being delivered from this place, devoted altogether to saving the Union without war, insurgent agents were in the city, seeking to destroy it without war—seeking to dissolve the Union and divide the effects by negotiation. Both parties deprecated war, but one of them would make war rather than let the nation survive, and the other would accept war rather than let it perish, and the war came. One-eighth of the whole population were colored slaves, not distributed generally over the Union, but localized in the Southern part of it. These slaves constituted a peculiar and powerful interest. All knew that this interest was somehow the cause of the war. To strengthen, perpetuate, and extend this interest was the object for which the insurgents would rend the Union by war, while the Government claimed no right to do more than to restrict the territorial enlargement of it.

Neither party expected for the war the magnitude or the duration which it has already attained. Neither anticipated that the cause of the conflict might cease, or even before the conflict itself should cease. Each looked for an easier triumph, and a result less fundamental and astounding.

Both read the same Bible and pray to the same God, and each invokes His aid against the other. It may seem strange that any men should dare to ask a just God's assistance in wringing their bread from the sweat of other men's faces, but let us judge not, that we be not judged. The prayer of both could not be answered. That of neither has been answered fully. The Almighty has His own purposes. Woe unto the world because of offences, for it must needs be that offences come, but woe to that man by whom the offence cometh. If we shall suppose that American slavery is one of these offences which, in the providence of God, must needs come, but which having continued through His appointed time, He now wills to remove, and that He gives to both North and South this terrible war as the woe due to those by whom the offence came, shall we discern there any departure from those Divine attributes which the believers in a living God always ascribe to Him? Fondly do we hope, fervently do we pray, that this mighty scourge of war may speedily pass away. Yet if God wills that it continue until all the wealth piled by the bondsman's two hundred and fifty years of unrequited toil shall be sunk, and until every drop of blood drawn with the lash shall be paid by another drawn with the sword, as was said three thousand years ago, so, still it must be said that the judgments of the Lord are true and righteous altogether.

With malice toward none, with charity for all, with firmness in the right as God gives us to see the right, let us finish the work we are in, to bind up the nation's wounds, to care for him who shall have borne the battle, and for his widow and his orphans, to do all which may achieve and cherish a just and a lasting peace among ourselves and with all nations.

SOURCE: *The Life and Public Services of Abraham Lincoln* by Henry J. Raymond (New York, 1865).

THOMAS MORRIS CHESTER

Three days before General Lee surrenders to General Grant at Appomatox, the black citizens of Richmond, Virginia, give President Lincoln a tremendous welcome, while white citizens look on. Thomas Chester, the son of black abolitionist parents in Harrisburg, Pennsylvania, is the war correspondent for The Philadelphia Press. *Assigned to Richmond, Chester reports on the events in the Confederate capital.*

DISPATCHES FROM RICHMOND

Hall of Congress

Richmond, April 4, 1865

. . . To Major General Godfrey Weitzel was assigned the duty of capturing Richmond. . . . Nothing occurred in the first part of the evening to awaken suspicion, though for the past few days it has been known to the authorities that the rebels, as I informed you, were evacuating the city. After midnight explosions began to occur so frequently as to confirm the evidence already in possession of the General-in-chief, that the last acts of an out-generalled army were in course of progress. The immense flames curling up throughout the rebel camps indicated that they were destroying all that could not be taken away.

The soldiers along the line gathered upon the breastworks to witness the scene and exchange congratulations. While thus silently gazing upon the columns of fire, one of the monster rams was exploded, which made the very earth tremble. If there was any doubt about the evacuation of Richmond that report banished them all. . . .

Brevet Brigadier General Draper's brigade of colored troops, Brevet Major General Kautz's division, were the first infantry to enter Richmond. The gallant 36th U. S. Colored Troops, under Lieutenant Colonel B. F. Pratt, has the honor of being the first regiment. . . .

In passing over the rebel works, we moved very cautiously in single file, for fear of exploding the innumerable torpedoes which were planted in front. So far as I can learn none has been exploded, and no one has been injured by those infernal machines. The soldiers were soon, under engineers, carefully digging them up and making the passage way beyond the fear of casualties.

Along the road which the troops marched, or rather double quicked, batches of negroes were gathered together testifying by unmistakable signs their delight at our coming. Rebel soldiers who had hid themselves when their army moved came out of the bushes, and gave themselves up as disgusted with the service. The haste of the rebels was evident in guns, camp equipage, telegraph wires, and other army property which they did not have time to burn.

. . . A scene was here witnessed which was not only grand, but sublime. Officers rushed into each other's arms, congratulating them upon the peaceful occupation of this citadel. Tears of joy ran down the faces of the more aged. The soldiers cheered lustily, which were mingled with every kind of expression of delight. The citizens stood gaping in wonder at the splendidly-equipped army marching along under the graceful folds of the old flag. Some waved their hats and women their hands in token of gladness. The pious old negroes, male and female, indulged in such expressions: "You've come at last"; "We've been looking for you these many days"; "Jesus has opened the way"; "God bless you"; "I've not seen that old flag for four years"; "It does my eyes good"; "Have you come to stay?"; "Thank God"; and similar expressions of exultation. The soldiers, black and white received these assurances of loyalty as evidences of the latent patriotism of an oppressed people, which a military despotism has not been able to crush. . . .

As we entered all the Government buildings were in flames, having been fired by order of the rebel General Ewall. The flames soon communicated themselves to the business part of the city, and continued to rage furiously throughout the day. All efforts to arrest this destructive element seemed for the best part of the day of no avail The fire department of Richmond rendered every aid, and to them and the co-operate labors of our soldiers belongs the credit of having saved Richmond from the devastating flames. As it is, all that part of the city lying between Ninth and Fourteenth streets, between Main street and the river inclusive, is in ruins. Among the most prominent buildings destroyed are the rebel War Department, Quartermaster General's Department, all the buildings with commissary stores, Shockoe's and Dibbrel's warehouses, well stored with tobacco, *Dispatch* and *Enquirer* newspaper buildings, the court house, (Guy) House, Farmers' Bank, Bank of Virginia, Exchange Bank, Tracers' Bank, American and Columbia hotels, and the Mayo bridge which unites Richmond with Manchester. The buildings of the largest merchants are among those which have been reduced to ashes. . . .

Hall of Congress

Richmond, April 6, 1865

The exultation of the loyal people of this city . . . is still being expressed by the most extravagant demonstrations of joy. The Union element in this city consists of negroes and poor whites, including all that have deserted from the army, or have survived the terrible exigencies which brought starvation to so many homes. As to the negroes, one thing is certain, that amid every disaster to our arms, amid the wrongs which they daily suffered for their known love for the Union, and amid the scourging which they received for trying to reach our army and enlist under our flag, they have ever prayed for the right cause, and testified their devotion to it in ten thousand instances, and especially in aiding our escaped prisoners to find our lines when to do so placed their own lives in peril.

The great event after the capture of the city was the arrival of President Lincoln in it. He came up to Rocket's wharf in one of Admiral Porter's vessels of war, and, with a file of sailors for a guard of honor, he walked up to Jeff Davis' house, the headquarters of General Weitzel. . . . [T]housands of persons had followed him to catch a sight of the Chief Magistrate of the United States. When he ascended the steps he faced the crowd and bowed his thanks for the prolonged exultation which was going up from that great concourse. The people seemed inspired by this acknowledgment, and with renewed vigor shouted louder and louder, until it seemed as if the echoes would reach the abode of those patriot spirits who had died without witnessing the sight.

. . . The President and party entered the mansion, where they remained for half an hour, the crowd still accumulating around it, when a headquarters' carriage was brought in front, drawn by four horses, and Mr. Lincoln, with his youngest son, Admiral Porter, General Kautz, and General Devin entered. . . . There is no describing the scene along the route. The colored population was wild with enthusiasm. Old men thanked God in a very boisterous manner, and old women shouted upon the pavement as high as they had ever done at a religious revival. But when the President passed through the Capitol yard it was filled with people. Washington's monument and the Capitol steps were one mass of humanity to catch a glimpse of him. . . .

Every one declares that Richmond never before presented such a spectacle of jubilee. It must be confessed that those who participated in this informal reception of the President were mainly negroes. There were many whites in the crowd, but they were lost in the great concourse of American citizens of African descent. Those who lived in the finest houses either stood motionless upon their steps or merely peeped through the window-blinds, with a very few exceptions. . . .

The people of Richmond, white and black, had been led to believe that when the Yankee army came its mission was one of plunder. But the orderly manner in which the soldiers have acted has undeceived them. The excitement is great, but nothing could be more orderly and decorous than the united crowds of soldiers and citizens. . . .

When the President returned to the flag-ship of Admiral Porter, in the evening, he was taken from the wharf in a cutter. Just as he pushed off, amid the cheering of the crowd, another good old colored female shouted out, "Don't drown, Massa Abe, for God's sake!"

The fire, which was nearly extinguished when I closed my last despatch, is entirely so now. Thousands of persons are gazing hourly with indignation upon the ruins. Gen. Lee ordered the evacuation of the city at an hour known to the remaining leaders of the rebellion, when Gens. Ewell and Breckinridge, and others, absconded, leaving orders with menials, robbers, and plunderers, kept together during the war by the "cohesive power of public plunder," to apply the torch to the different tobacco warehouses, public buildings, arsenals, stores, flour mills, powder magazines, and every important place of deposit. A south wind prevailed, and the flames spread with devastating effect. . . . In short, Secession was burnt out. . . .

SOURCE: *The Press* (Philadelphia)
April 11 and April 15, 1865.

HENRY TIMROD

Just after the war and the last of the funerals and before the people had time or resources to erect the Civil War monuments that would be a part of countless cities and towns North and South, Confederate poet Henry Timrod writes these verses. This poem was put to music and sung at the decoration of the graves of the Confederate dead in Magnolia Cemetery, Charleston, South Carolina, in 1866.

ODE

I

Sleep sweetly in your humble graves,
Sleep, martyrs of a fallen cause;
Though yet no marble column craves
The pilgrim here to pause.

II

In seeds of laurel in the earth
The blossom of your fame is blown,
And somewhere, waiting for its birth,
The shaft is in the stone!

III

Meanwhile, behalf the tardy years
Which keep in trust your storied tombs,
Behold! your sisters bring their tears,
And these memorial blooms.

IV

Small tributes! but your shades will smile
More proudly on these wreaths today,
Than when some cannon-moulded pile
Shall overlook this bay.

V

Stoop, angels, hither from the skies!
There is no holier spot of ground
Than where defeated valor lies,
  By mourning beauty crowned!

SOURCE: *War Poetry of the South,*
edited by William Gilmore Simms
(New York, 1867).

JOURDON ANDERSON

*The critical role of black workers in the South's economic
life is indirectly evident in the following letter dictated by
a black man who liberated himself and his family from
slavery before the end of the war. Asked by his former
"owner" to return now that the war is over and work
for wages, Jourdon Anderson, in rejecting the invitation,
gives a richly ironic comparison of life in slavery and life
in freedom.*

LETTER FROM A FREEDMAN TO
HIS OLD MASTER

DAYTON, Ohio, August 7, 1865.

To my Old Master, Col. P. H. Anderson, *Big Spring, Tennessee.*

SIR: I got your letter and was glad to find that you had not forgotten Jordan, and that you wanted me to come back and live with you
again, promising to do better for me than anybody else can. I have
often felt uneasy about you. I thought the Yankees would have hung
you long before this, for harboring Rebs. they found at your house. I
suppose they never heard about your going to Col. Martin's to kill the
Union soldier that was left by his company in their stable. Although
you shot at me twice before I left you, I did not want to hear of your
being hurt, and am glad you are still living. It would do me good to go
back to the dear old home again and see Miss Mary and Miss Martha
and Allen, Esther, Green, and Lee. Give my love to them all, and tell
them I hope we will meet in the better world, if not in this. I would
have gone back to see you all when I was working in the Nashville
Hospital, but one of the neighbors told me Henry intended to shoot
me if he ever got a chance.

I want to know particularly what the good chance is you propose to give me. I am doing tolerably well here; I get $25 a month, with victuals and clothing; have a comfortable home for Mandy (the folks here call her Mrs. Anderson). [A]nd the children, Milly Jane, and Grundy, go to school and are learning well; the teacher says Grundy has a head for a preacher. They go to Sunday-School, and Mandy and me attend church regularly. We are kindly treated; sometimes we overhear others saying, "Them colored people were slaves" down in Tennessee. The children feel hurt when they hear such remarks, but I tell them it was no disgrace in Tennessee to belong to Col. Anderson. Many darkeys would have been proud, as I used to was, to call you master. Now, if you will write and say what wages you will give me, I will be better able to decide whether it would be to my advantage to move back again.

As to my freedom, which you say I can have, there is nothing to be gained on that score, as I got my free-papers in 1864 from the Provost-Marshal-General of the Department at Nashville. Mandy says she would be afraid to go back without some proof that you are sincerely disposed to treat us justly and kindly—and we have concluded to test your sincerity by asking you to send us our wages for the time we served you. This will make us forget and forgive old sores, and rely on your justice and friendship in the future. I served you faithfully for thirty-two years, and Mandy twenty years, at $25 a month for me, and $2 a week for Mandy. Our earnings would amount to $11,680. Add to this the interest for the time our wages has been kept back and deduct what you paid for our clothing and three doctor's visits to me, and pulling a tooth for Mandy, and the balance will show what we are in justice entitled to. Please send the money by Adams Express, in care of V. Winters, esq., Dayton, Ohio. If you fail to pay us for faithful labors in the past we can have little faith in your promises in the future. We trust the good Maker has opened your eyes to the wrongs which you and your fathers have done to me and my fathers, in making us toil for you for generations without recompense. Here I draw my wages every Saturday night, but in Tennessee there was never any pay day for the negroes any more than for the horses and cows. Surely there will be a day of reckoning for those who defraud the laborer of his hire.

In answering this letter please state if there would be any safety for my Milly and Jane, who are now grown up and both good looking girls. You know how it was with poor Matilda and Catherine. I would rather stay here and starve and die if it come to that than have my girls brought to shame by the violence and wickedness of their young masters. You will also please state if there has been any schools opened for the colored children in your neighborhood, the great desire of my life now is to give my children an education, and have them form virtuous habits.

From your old servant,   JOURDON ANDERSON.

P.S.—Say howdy to George Carter, and thank him for taking the pistol from you when you were shooting at me.

SOURCE: *New York Daily Tribune,*
August 22, 1865.

BIBLIOGRAPHY

Anderson, Jourdon. "Letter from a Freedman to His Old Master," *New York Daily Tribune*, August 22, 1865.

Anonymous. "Letter, Dec. 17, 1864," *Pickett and His Men* by LaSalle Corbell Pickett, Atlanta: Foote and Davies Co., 1899.

Anonymous. "War Diary of a Union Woman in the South," in *Strange True Stories of Louisiana*, ed. George Washington Cable. New York: Scribners, 1889.

Ballou, Major Sullivan. "Letters, 1861," Ballou Correspondence, Rhode Island Historical Society Library, mss. 277.

Barziza, Decimus et Ultimus. *The Adventures of a Prisoner of War; and Life and Scenes in Federal Prisons: Johnson's Island, Fort Delaware, and Point Lookout; by an Escaped Prisoner of Hood's Texas Brigade*. Houston: Richardson and Owen's, 1865.

Blackford, Susan Leigh Colston, compiler. *Memoirs of Life In and Out of the Army in Virginia During the War Between the States*. Annotated and edited by her husband, Charles Minor Blackford. Lynchburg, Va.: J.P. Bell Co., 1894–96. 2 vols.

Burge, Dolly Sumner Lunt. American Women's Diaries, 1789–1923. Microfilm. Manuscripts and Archives, Yale University Library.

Chester, Thomas. "Richmond, April 4 and April 6, 1865," *The Press* (Philadelphia), April 11 and April 15, 1865.

Child, L. Maria. *The Right Way The Safe Way, Proved by Emancipation in the British West Indies, and Elsewhere*. New York: 5 Beekman Street, 1862.

Davis, Jefferson. "Speech, Columbia, South Carolina, October 6, 1864," in *Jefferson Davis, Constitutionalist: His Letters, Papers and Speeches*, ed. Dunbar Rowland. Jackson: Mississippi Department of Archives and History, 1923.

Dawson, Sarah Morgan. *A Confederate Girl's Diary*. Boston: Houghton Mifflin Co., 1913.

"Declaration of Wrongs and Rights Made by the Colored Men of the United States of America in Convention Assembled in Syracuse, N.Y., Oct. 4, 1864," *Proceedings of the National Convention of Colored Men, held in the City of Syracuse, N.Y., Oct. 4, 5, 6, and 7, 1864; with the Bill of Wrongs and Rights, and the Address to the American People*. Boston: G. C. Rand & Avery, 1864.

Dickinson, Emily. *Poems*, ed. Mabel Loomis Todd and T. W. Higginson. Boston: Roberts Brothers, 1892.

147

Dickinson, Emily. *Letters of Emily Dickinson*, ed. Mabel Loomis Todd. Boston: Roberts Brothers, 1894.

Douglass, Frederick. "Substance of a Lecture Delivered by Frederick Douglass, at Zion Church, Sunday, June 30," *Douglass' Monthly*, August 1861.

Douglass, Frederick. "Speech of Frederick Douglass on the War," *Douglass' Monthly*, February 1862.

Douglass, Lewis. "Letter to Amelia, July 20, 1863," Library of Congress, Carter Woodson Papers, 1054.

Edmonds, Sarah. *Nurse and Spy in the Union Army*. Hartford: W.S. Williams & Co., 1865.

Forten, Charlotte. "Life on the Sea Islands," *Atlantic Monthly*, June 1864.

Gideon. "Slavery and State Sovereignty," *Charleston Daily Courier*, January 24, 1865.

Gilbert, John. "Letter, Feb. 4, 1862," Letters of John Gilbert, New Hampshire Historical Society, mss. 1900-001.

Gooding, Corporal James Henry. "Corporal James Henry Gooding to Abraham Lincoln, 28 Sept. 1863," National Archives, enclosed in [Harper & Brothers] to [Abraham Lincoln], 12 Oct. 1863, H-133, 1863 Letters Received, ser. 360, Colored Troops Division, RG 94 [B-408].

Harris, Emily and David Golightly. *Piedmont Farmer: The Journals of David Golightly Harris*, ed. Philip N. Racine. Knoxville, Tenn.: University of Tennessee Press, 1990.

Heiskell, Jim. "Affidavit of a Tennessee Fugitive Slave," *Freedom: A Documentary History of Emancipation*, Sr. 1, Vol. 1, eds. Ira Berlin, et al. Cambridge: Cambridge University Press, 1982.

Jacobs, Harriet. *Incidents in the Life of a Slave Girl*. Written by Herself. Edited by L. Maria Child. Boston: Published for the Author, 1861.

Johnson, Hannah. "Hannah Johnson to Hon. Mr. Lincoln, 31 July 1863," National Archives, J-17 1863, Letters Received, ser. 360, Colored Troops Division, RG 94 [B-34].

Jones, J. B. *A Rebel War Clerk's Diary At The Confederate States Capital*. Philadelphia: J.B. Lippincott and Co., 1866.

Lincoln, Abraham. *The Life and Public Services of Abraham Lincoln, Sixteenth President of the United States; together with His State Papers, including His Speeches, Addresses, Messages, Letters, and Proclamations, and the Closing Scenes Connected with his Life and Death* by Henry J. Raymond. New York: Derby and Miller, Publishers, 1865.

Lindsay, J. W. "Testimony of J. W. Lindsay, St. Catharine's, 1863," National Archives, American Freedman's Inquiry Commission, Canadian Testimony, filed with 0-328-1863, RG 94 [M-619].

Logue, Sarah. "Letter to Rev. J. W. Loguen, from His Old Mistress," *The Liberator*, April 27, 1860.

Loguen, J. W. "Mr. Loguen's Reply," *The Liberator*, April 27, 1860.

Loughborough, Mary Ann (Webster). *My Cave Life in Vicksburg with Letters of Trial and Travel*. New York: D. Appleton & Co., 1864.

McPherson, Surgeon J.B. et al. "Surgeon J. B. McPherson et al. to President Abraham Lincoln," [Feb. 1864], National Archives, M-118 1864, Letters Received, ser. 360, Colored Troops Division, RG 94 [B-11].

Melville, Herman. *Battle-Pieces and Aspects of the War*. New York: Harper & Brothers, Publishers, 1866.

Mills, Luther Rice. *Letters of Luther Rice Mills: A Confederate Soldier*, ed. George D. Harmon. Raleigh: North Carolina Historical Review, July 1927. Reprint.

Moseley, John. "Letter, July 4, 1863," in *Soldiers Blue and Grey* by James L. Robertson, Jr. Columbia: University of South Carolina Press, 1988.

Palmer, The Reverend Benjamin. "Thanksgiving Sermon, November 29, 1860," *The Life and Letters of Benjamin Morgan Palmer* by Thomas Cary Johnson. Richmond, Virginia: Presbyterian Committee of Publication, 1906.

Pickett, General George E. *The Heart of a Soldier*. New York: Seth Moyle, 1913.

Purvis, Robert. "Speech of Robert Purvis, Esq." *The Liberator*, May 22, 1863.

Remond, Sarah Parker. "The Negroes in the United States of America," in *Lift Every Voice: African American Oratory, 1787–1900*, eds. Philip S. Foner and Robert James Branham. Tuscaloosa: University of Alabama Press, 1998.

Rice, Private Spotswood. "From Your Father Spotswood Rice to Mary Ann Corra," [3 Sept. 1864], National Archives enclosed in F.W. Diggs to Genl. Rosecrans, 10 Sept. 1864, D-296 1864, Letters Received, ser. 2593, Dept. of the MO, RG 393 Pt. 1 [C-154].

Statts, Mrs. "Wm. Henry Nichols," *Report of the Committee of Merchants for the Relief of Colored People Suffering from the Late Riots in the City of New York*. New York: George A. Whitehorne, 1863.

Thomas, Ella Gertrude Clanton. *The Secret Eye: The Journal of Ella Gertrude Clanton Thomas*, ed. Virginia Ingraham Burr. Chapel Hill: University of North Carolina Press, 1990.

Timrod, Henry. *War Poetry of the South*, ed. William Gilmore Simms. New York: Richardson and Company, 1867.

Ware, The Reverend John F. W. *Our Duty Under Reverse: A Sermon Preached in the Church of the Cambridgeport Parish, Sunday, 28 July, 1861*. Boston: John Wilson and Son, 1861.

Wears, Isaiah C. "Lincoln's Colonization Proposal Is Anti-Christian," *Lift Every Voice: African American Oratory, 1787–1900*, eds. Philip S. Foner and Robert James Branham. Tuscaloosa: University of Alabama Press, 1998.

Whitman, Walt. *Leaves of Grass*. Philadelphia: David McKay, 1883.

Woodson, Sarah J. "Address to the Youth," *The Semi-Centenary and the Retrospection of the African Methodist Episcopal Church in the United States of America*, ed. Daniel A. Payne. Baltimore: Sherwood and Co., 1866.

INDEX

Printed and bound by CPI Group (UK) Ltd, Croydon, CR0 4YY

09/06/2025

14686107-0003